D1217110

Neil Caplan

The Lausanne Conference, 1949

A Case Study in Middle East Peacemaking

OCCASIONAL PAPERS

The papers in this series represent the findings of fellows of the Moshe Dayan Center or researchers from other institutions. The opinions expressed in this series are those of the authors and should not be construed as representing those of the Moshe Dayan Center.

All references to these papers should be properly acknowledged.

Neil Caplan

The Lausanne Conference, 1949

A Case Study in Middle East Peacemaking

Tel Aviv University

The Moshe Dayan Center for
Middle Eastern and African Studies

The publication of this research was supported by The Bronfman Program for the Study of Arab-Jewish Relations.

Design and production: Ruth Beth-Or

ISBN 965-224-013-3

In memory of
Professor **Elie Kedourie**,
a teacher whose impact
on his students
was more than he imagined

CONTENTS

Preface 7
Abbreviations 9
Introduction 11
Third-Party Intervention:
The United Nations and the United States / 11
Two Tracks and Resolution 194 / 14
Learning from Failure / 16
Chapter 1: Pre-Negotiation 19
Getting Down to Work / 19
Shuttle Diplomacy / 20
Quest for an Advance Gesture from Israel / 23
Chapter 2: PCC Beirut Conference, March 1949 26
Chapter 3: Towards Lausanne:
Continuing Pressure for an Israeli Gesture 32
The Shadow of Rhodes / 38
Strains in the Arab Common Front / 40
Chapter 4: Opening the Conference 43
Maneuvering for Position / 43
Structures and Procedures / 47
Chapter 5: A Basis for Discussion:
The Lausanne Protocol, 12 May 1949 51
Staking Out the Positions: The First Deadlock / 54
Chapter 6: Attempts to Break the Deadlock:
Israel's Gaza Offer 60
Presidential Rebuke to Israel / 60
Israel's Offer to Incorporate the Gaza Strip / 61
American Good Offices Offered to Israel and Egypt / 65
Chapter 7: June Stalemate and Adjournment 70
Chapter 8: Activity during the Recess 75
Fine-tuning of the American, Israeli and Arab Positions / 75
Pursuing the Gaza Proposal / 78
The British Eight-Point Plan / 86

Chapter 9: Resumption of the Conference 89
Israel's Offer to Repatriate 100,000 Refugees / 92
Chapter 10: Continued Conciliation or Imposed Settlement? 96
Chapter 11: Winding up the Conference: The PCC Questionnaire and the Economic Survey Mission 104
Chapter 12: Lausanne Postscripts 111
New York Meetings / 111
Lobbying the State Department / 114
Chapter 13: Conclusions 118
The Attitudes and Positions of the Parties / 119
The Ineffectiveness of the PCC / 124
The US Role / 131
Notes 139
Sources and Bibliography 170
Index 175

PREFACE

Prior to the Madrid Conference of late 1991 and its follow-ups in Washington and elsewhere, the Lausanne Conference of April — September 1949 and the brief, ceremonial Geneva Conference of December 1973 stood out as the only occasions on which Israel and the Arab states were assembled together for peace talks. The Lausanne Conference — despite its failure — offers lessons as an important effort to discuss a comprehensive solution to what was then an early stage of today's much more complicated and intractable Arab-Israeli conflict. Like Rhodes and the more familiar Camp David, Lausanne has come to signify not just a venue for past negotiations, but also a code word denoting an entire peace process. Lausanne also represented an outcome that subsequently became a reference point or milestone to each of the parties who attended.

Despite its central importance to the diplomatic history of the Arab-Israeli dispute, there has been, to date, no scholarly monograph devoted exclusively to the Lausanne Conference. The present work is part of a larger project studying international attempts to promote Arab-Israeli negotiations between 1948 and 1956. I wish to express my gratitude to the government of Quebec, the Canadian Institute for International Peace and Security, and the Memorial Foundation for Jewish Culture for the generous financial support without which this work would not have been possible. Research was conducted in Israel as a Fellow of the Moshe Dayan Center for Middle Eastern and African Studies of Tel Aviv University, and in England as a visiting scholar of the Oxford Centre for Postgraduate Hebrew Studies. I am deeply indebted to each of these institutions for providing its own distinctive setting, hospitality and opportunities for research and discussion with colleagues. My warmest thanks are due to Dr. Asher Susser, Amira Margalit and Edna Liftman of the Dayan Center for their support and encouragement.

After spending so many months ordering and poring over quantities of files, newspapers, periodicals, clippings and books in various archives and libraries, I have accumulated a heavy debt of gratitude to the staffs and directors of the following institutions (alphabetically) for their helpfulfulness in dealing with my many requests: Ben-Gurion Archive (BGA), Sde Boqer; Dr. Yoram Mayorek, Central Zionist Archives (CZA), Jerusalem; Anat Rapoport and Haim Gal, Dayan Center Documentation Center, Library and Press Archives, Tel Aviv University; Dr. Philip Mattar, Institute for Palestine Studies, Washington; Dr.

Moshe Mossek, Dr. Yehoshua Freundlich and Yemima Rosenthal, Israel State Archives (ISA), Jerusalem; Kressel Collection and Library, Yarnton, Oxford; Public Record Office (PRO), Kew, England; St. Antony's College, Middle East Centre Library, Oxford; Marilla B. Guptil, United Nations Archives (UNA), New York; United States National Archives (USNA), Washington DC; and Washington National Records Center (WNRC), Suitland MD. Special thanks are also due to Dr. Kamal Abdel-Malek, Dina Cohen and Fawwaz Gerges, for their assistance with Arabic materials, and to Dr. Bryna Bogoch and Benjamin Caplan for their exccellent work in gathering research materials.

Neil Caplan
Humanities Department
Vanier College, Montreal, Canada

August 1993

ABBREVIATIONS

BGA = Ben-Gurion Archives, Sde Boqer

CZA = Central Zionist Archives, Jerusalem

FO = Foreign Office, London

FRUS = *Foreign Relations of the United States*

GAA = General Armistice Agreement (1949)

HMG = His Majesty's Government, United Kingdom

ID = *Documents on the Foreign Policy of Israel*

IDF = Israel Defense Forces

IMFA = Israel Ministry of Foreign Affairs

ISA = Israel State Archives, Jerusalem

IsrDel = Israel Delegation

IsrEmb = Israel Embassy

MFA = Ministry of Foreign Affairs

NSC = National Security Council

PCC = Palestine Conciliation Commission (= United Nations Conciliation Commission for Palestine)

PGI = Provisional Government of Israel (May 1948 — January 1949)

PRO = Public Record Office, Kew, England

UKEmb = United Kingdom Embassy

UN = United Nations

UNA = United Nations Archives, New York

UNGA = United Nations General Assembly

UNSC = United Nations Security Council

UNTSO = United Nations Truce Supervisory Organization

USDel = US Delegation

USDiv = US Division, Israel Ministry of Foreign Affairs

USEmb = United States Embassy

USNA = National Archives, Washington DC

USSD = United States, Department of State

WNRC = Washington National Records Center
E/C/G = Egypt/Cairo/General Correspondence

INTRODUCTION

Third-Party Intervention: The United Nations and the United States

One of the distinguishing features of the Arab-Israeli conflict is its dynamic of moving, to use Nadav Safran's phrase, "from war to war," rather than following the normally expected transition from war to armistice to peace. Following the conclusion of the 1947-1949 military struggle which saw the end of the Palestine mandate and the birth of the State of Israel, the United States, Great Britain and the United Nations found themselves involved in efforts to manage or resolve the latest manifestations of a generations-old dispute. Most of this third-party involvement in the Arab-Israeli conflict in the wake of 1948 could be classified as attempts at *conflict management*, the objective of which was generally the avoidance of a resumption of military action: keeping tension down, investigating and resolving localized grievances, avoiding frontier flare-ups, preventing reprisals, and calling for and monitoring cease-fires.

Yet there were also examples of more ambitious third-party involvement which aimed at *conflict resolution*, in an attempt to alter the *status quo* and produce a settlement upon which all parties could agree. The main difficulty of moving from war to armistice to peace was the fundamental gap separating the two parties. Israel, after the trauma of surviving its war of independence, was relatively satisfied with the postwar *status quo*. The Arab states, still in a state of shock over the unexpectedly lopsided Israeli victory, remained fundamentally opposed to the creation of the Jewish state and hoped to undo many of the new realities created by the November 1947 UN partition resolution and the ensuing fighting. While individual

Arab regimes were willing to launch, or respond to, secret feelers for peace with Israel, none of these bilateral probes resulted in any of the armistice agreements being converted into a peace treaty.[1]

The United Nations became involved in both the conflict management and conflict-resolution efforts, registering relatively more success at the former (peacekeeping) than at the latter (peacemaking).[2] Behind the scenes, the Western powers — particularly the United States — played a crucial role in both UN peacekeeping and peacemaking. In the latter sphere, the UN General Assembly (UNGA) created a Conciliation Commission for Palestine (or Palestine Conciliation Commission, hereinafter: PCC) and mandated that body to engage in conciliation and (some argued) mediation with representatives of Israel and the Arab states in the wake of the 1948-49 war. But, as any student of international organizations will attest, the moral authority of an organ operating under UN auspices is not, in itself, enough to coax or cajole the main protagonists into offering their full cooperation in peacemaking activities. The role of the powers is all-important. As one scholar has recently argued, the behind-the-scenes involvement of the US in establishing the PCC was "a historic turning point at which the Americans replaced the British as the peace brokers." Through their actions during the coming year, the Americans would become "the prime movers of the peace process" undertaken by the Commission.[3]

Throughout 1949, the United States sought, on behalf of the PCC, to exert its leverage on the parties in dispute. American involvement in the conciliation effort took various forms, including:

a. making "diplomatic representations" behind closed doors, a relatively mild method of exerting pressure by offering friendly advice, or expressing concern, about Israeli or Arab behavior considered to be unhelpful to the peace process;
b. offering or withholding international diplomatic support for Israel or an Arab state inside and outside the UN;
c. threatening to withhold economic assistance, in an attempt to encourage cooperative behavior on the part of the parties;

d. offering Egypt and Israel its "good offices" for convening direct talks to consider the latter's proposal to take back and annex the Gaza Strip (conquered and held by Egypt in the war) and resettle its refugee population inside Israel.

None of these interventions was crowned with major successes, and the overall conciliation effort headed for failure by the close of the summer of 1949.

In preparing Mark Ethridge to serve as US representative on the PCC, Acting Secretary of State Robert Lovett in mid-January outlined the basic positions of the US government on the various issues. Ethridge was asked to bear the following in mind in the event that he would be called upon to express the views of his government regarding the territorial lines of an Arab-Israeli settlement:

1. No modification should be made in the boundaries of the State of Israel as established by the General Assembly resolution of 29 November 1947, without the full consent of the State of Israel.
2. If Israel desires additions to its territory as defined under the 29 November resolution, i.e., areas allotted by the General Assembly to the Arabs such as western Galilee and Jaffa, now under Israeli occupation, Israel should make territorial concessions elsewhere, i.e., the southern Negev. Israel is not entitled to keep both the Negev and western Galilee and Jaffa. If there is no agreement between the parties, the Israelis should relinquish western Galilee and Jaffa and the Arabs should relinquish the Israeli portion of the Negev.
3. If Israel desires to retain western Galilee and Jaffa, the southern border of Israel should not be drawn further south than the thirty-first parallel within the territory allotted to Israel under the resolution of 29 November.

This was a restatement of what was to become known as the "Jessup principle" — an American proposal for an exchange of territory enunciated several months earlier by Philip C. Jessup at the United Nations. If the parties should, in the end, fail to reach agreement,

Ethridge would "be authorized to join with the other members of the Commission in an effort to persuade the parties to agree upon the frontiers" as outlined above. The US, Lovett added, was also planning to coordinate its efforts with the British government in an "attempt to induce the parties to reach agreement on this basis."[4]

The Americans would discover during the Lausanne experience that few of their representations, exhortations or expressions of disappointment had any major effect in moving the deadlocked parties towards compromise and agreement. But, when faced with this realization, and in spite of the admirable clarity of Lovett's instructions to Ethridge, the State Department would prove unable or unwilling to take responsibility for promoting a settlement based on these — or any other — precise territorial arrangements.

Two Tracks and Resolution 194

By January 1949, the United Nations had set up two complementary but separate tracks for promoting a peaceful adjustment of the conflict over Palestine. The "Rhodes track" was based upon Security Council (UNSC) resolution 62 (1948) of 16 November 1948, which called upon the parties "to seek agreement forthwith, by negotiations conducted either directly or through the acting mediator, with a view to the immediate establishment of [an] armistice."[5] The Israeli-Egyptian talks begun at Rhodes on 13 January would be followed by similar talks involving Lebanon, Jordan and (after some interruption and delay) Syria.

The second track — which would lead to Lausanne — took as its starting point UNGA resolution 194(III) of 11 December 1948. This resolution, the culmination of lengthy debates surrounding the September report of the late mediator, Count Folke Bernadotte, established the PCC and mandated that body, *inter alia,* to "take steps to assist the Governments and authorities concerned to achieve a final settlement of all questions outstanding between them." The resolution also called upon Israel and the Arab states

> to extend the scope of negotiations provided for in the Security Council's resolution of 16 November 1948 and to seek agreement by negotiations conducted either with the Conciliation Commission or directly, with a view to the final settlement of all questions outstanding between them.[6]

The phrase "either with the Conciliation Commission or directly" reflected the *impasse* created by the Arab states' hardening position against direct dealings with the newly-created Jewish state. The practical outcome was that the PCC, while paying lip service to the possibility and desirability of direct Arab-Israeli talks, assumed the role of go-between, or "postman," between parties in conflict who would never meet around the same table. A second underlying ambiguity in the PCC's role and mandate was whether it was to undertake "conciliation" in the narrow sense, dealing only with proposals put forth by the parties themselves; or, whether, as inheritor of the functions of the late Count Bernadotte, its functions should properly include "mediation" in a broader sense — i.e., the ability to propose its own peace plans for the consideration of the parties in dispute. Although some, in retrospect, would wish it had chosen the latter course, the PCC followed a strong State Department lead during its Lausanne effort by restricting its role to conciliator in the narrow sense.

Like the better known UNSC resolution 242 of 1967, UNGA resolution 194 of December 1948 soon became a benchmark, frequently invoked during the coming months and years as an authority on which to base a whole range of claims and complaints. Shortly after passage of the resolution, the governments of the United States, France and Turkey designated representatives to sit on the newly-formed Conciliation Commission. Chairmanship was to be rotated among the three on a monthly basis. Following the recommendations of this historic resolution, the main task before the commission was to seek agreement between Arabs and Israelis regarding (a) the return of Palestinian refugees who had fled or had been expelled from their homes during the 1947-1948 fighting, (b) the final delimitation of the boundaries of the new Israeli state, and (c) the establishment of an international regime for Jerusalem. The latter item would be relegated to a subcommittee operating separately from the overall peace effort at Lausanne.

Learning from Failure

The success of Acting Mediator Ralph Bunche at Rhodes stands in stark contrast to the PCC's failure at Lausanne. The memoirs of participants and contemporary observers are fairly unanimous in heaping scorn on the quality of the PCC's personnel and methods while expressing high praise for Ralph Bunche's personal talents and skills. The fact that the latter sought to achieve limited armistice agreements while the former was left to resolve the deeper political contradictions between Arabs and Israelis is perhaps not given sufficient weight by those who have invoked the comparison. We shall return to this question in our final assessment.

Despite the absence of a successful outcome to what may be called the Lausanne peace process, there is much to be learned from a closer look at the failed attempt. This learning can be of two kinds: practical and academic. Since there is a high degree of continuity in the basic positions of the protagonists and in the kinds of opportunities that arise for contacts and diplomacy, practitioners of current and future negotiations may benefit from knowing how parties acted and reacted under the specific circumstances of the Lausanne effort. Of course, Arab-Israeli diplomacy is nothing like an exact science, and there is no guarantee that studying the lessons of the past will assure future success. There are just too many uncontrolled variables that must be taken into account, such as the changing domestic political situation within Israel and each of the Arab states, the perceived balance of military advantage, and the interests of world powers. Circumstances never reproduce themselves identically; nor can parties be brought into negotiating situations under controlled laboratory conditions.

Still, there is much to be gained — perhaps more in terms

of narrowing options of what may, or may not, work — from systematic attempts to draw lessons from past negotiating experience. Successful blending of practical and academic experience in this field is, unfortunately, all too rare.[7] Some historians have rightly criticized political leaders and would-be mediators for not taking the time and care to equip themselves with a solid understanding of the good and bad experiences of their predecessors' attempts at resolving this long-festering dispute.[8] Readers who have not already discovered it elsewhere will be struck by the repetitiveness of certain situations and patterns of behavior exhibited by the main protagonists and third parties alike. Those familiar with the relatively successful Camp David (1978) and Madrid/Washington (1991-92) peace processes may be tempted, after reading the following account, to draw some comparisons regarding the limitations and failures experienced by the United States in its earlier role as "peace broker" at Lausanne.

A second type of learning that can be gained from a careful study of failed attempts such as Lausanne is a more accurate understanding of the true dynamics of the broader Arab-Israeli conflict. By examining the behind-the-scenes calculations and motives of the parties as they face the prospect of negotiating situations, one becomes better able to distinguish between their highly-developed advocacy, propaganda and posturing, on the one hand, and their equally skillful tactical maneuvering in pursuit of specific political goals, on the other. Through a case study like Lausanne, the reader may develop a better appreciation of the complex mixture of emotional and rational components of each party's stance.

CHAPTER 1

Pre-Negotiation

Getting Down to Work

Even before the conclusion of the Israeli-Egyptian armistice talks, the PCC began its work in February 1949, attempting to prepare the ground for a peace settlement in accordance with the terms of its mandate under resolution 194.[1] Although it was spread over five months — rather than six weeks, as at Rhodes — the PCC's Lausanne effort followed a similar course, beginning with pre-negotiation and involving, throughout, recurring deadlocks and appeals to the US for assistance in the role of outside enforcer.

From the start, the PCC's work style included two parallel channels of communication with Arabs and Israelis:

a. formal meetings with Arab or Israeli representatives. These usually involved all three commissioners. Formal demands or replies would be submitted and discussed following informal preparatory sessions. There were no joint Arab-Israeli meetings held under PCC auspices.
b. informal, off-the-record talks. These often involved only one commissioner and/or staff member at a time. Most of the real attempts at persuasion and conciliation were made during these sessions.

This two-track style afforded much flexibility, but also occasional confusion which would have to be straightened out in working sessions attended only by the commissioners and members of the PCC secretariat.

The activities of the PCC surrounding the Lausanne conference can be broken down into the following stages:

1. Pre-negotiation (February-April 1949)
2. Formal opening sessions (late April)
3. Signing the Lausanne Protocol (12 May 1949), followed by incompatible Arab and Israeli offers
4. Recess (1-18 July)
5. Return to Lausanne (19 July), followed by Israel's offer to repatriate 100,000 refugees
6. PCC questionnaire, deadlock and adjournment (August-September)
7. Postscripts: New York and Washington (October-November).

Shuttle Diplomacy

On 7 February 1949, the PCC held its first informal talks in the Middle East. The commission hoped that a "preliminary exchange of views" with Moshe Shertok (later Sharett) and his aides in Jerusalem would facilitate its scheduled discussions in Arab capitals. By all accounts, this five-hour session was not an encouraging one for either side. The meeting began with the exposition of diametrically opposed views on the internationalization of Jerusalem. On the issue of refugees, Foreign Minister Shertok repeated his government's view that the problem could "only be settled as part of [a] peace settlement" and that there could be "no significant return of refugees before and possibly after that event." Israel would recognize its obligation to pay compensation for abandoned property. As to a peace settlement, Shertok indicated Israel's preference for separate treaties with each neighbor, and did not wish a "general conference." On the issue of boundaries, he stated that the annexation of Arab Palestine to Transjordan (soon to be known as Jordan) would invalidate Israel's previous acceptance of the November 1947 UN partition resolution. In response to a request, the foreign minister promised to provide the PCC with a memorandum outlining his government's views on the refugee question; the request was fulfilled only six weeks later.[2]

The commissioners were reportedly "offended" as they listened to Shertok's statements regarding the refugees, feeling that Shertok had "insulted [the] intelligence" of the commission with a repetition of his 15 November 1948 speech in the UNGA. Ethridge was personally "astonished" at these Israeli attitudes, in view of the "imperative necessity for friendly relations." While the PCC representative believed that it might, in the end, prove necessary to resettle the "greater proportion" of Arab refugees in the neighboring Arab states, he felt it was "contrary to Israel's best interest at [the] outset to take [an] inhuman position."[3]

Initial Arab reaction to the activities of the PCC was, on the surface, more hopeful and positive. The Syrian prime minister, Khalid al-Azm, welcomed this "new approach to [the] Palestine problem," hoping it would result "in some satisfactory settlement more in keeping with [the] principles of right and justice than has heretofore been evident." In a conversation with the American minister in Damascus, the Syrian leader decried Israel's "aggressive tactics" and its repeated "flaunt[ing]" of UN resolutions, but suggested that "some conciliatory gesture"

> which might take the form of [a] public statement by [the] Israeli Prime Minister that if [the] armistice were accepted by all parties Israel will withdraw [its] forces in accordance with UNSC resolutions [of 4 and 16 November] as [a] preliminary to boundaries negotiations, would doubtless help [the] embarrassed Arabs such as Syria and Iraq to save face and might ease [the] way for [a] negotiated settlement through [the] Good Offices of [the] PCC.[4]

The Iraqi foreign minister was more cynical about the latest UN effort, pointing to the need for the US to prove its "good faith towards [the]Arabs" by "putting pressure on Israel" to accept the right of refugees to return and to allow Jerusalem to "remain [an]Arab city."[5]

The PCC began its official tour in Transjordan, where it met Prime Minister Tawfiq Abu al-Huda on 11 February and learned of that country's preference for separate peace talks, even if these were objected to by other Arab states. Abu al-Huda also openly indicated his country's interest in having land access to the eastern Mediterranean through Gaza.[6] More intensive meetings were held in Cairo between 13-15 February. The Egyptian foreign minister tentatively indicated Egypt's preference for "direct negotiations" as opposed to a general peace conference, but added that "Egypt would have to wait to see if Israel wanted peace and would abide by SC resolutions."[7] While elaborating Egypt's firm position on the return of the Palestinian refugees, both he and Prime Minister Ibrahim Abd al-Hadi, in separate meetings, took the opportunity to add complaints about Israel's "intransigent line" being taken at the Rhodes armistice negotiations.[8] These remarks seem to have impressed Ethridge, who made a special appeal to the State Department to seek a breakthrough at Rhodes by exerting greater pressure on Israel.[9] But the commissioners were also dissatisfied with the Egyptians, whom they accused of "failing to impart frankly and fully what was in their mind regarding the final settlement." Their impression, they reported to British Ambassador Sir Ronald Campbell, was that the Egyptians were using the refugee issue as a maneuver to gain time and postpone the necessity of signing a final agreement which would, in effect, admit Egyptian defeat.[10]

The PCC's tour of Arab capitals concluded with stops in Saudi Arabia (16-17 February), Iraq (18-19 February), Syria (21 February) and Lebanon (23 February). According to one experienced British diplomat, the tour had "brought the commission up against the realities" and had "removed a number of their previous misconceptions."[11] As ideas for a settlement began to gel in Ethridge's reports to the State Department, Secretary of State Dean Acheson was forced to caution him:

> Our thought has always been that [the] PCC should initially endeavor to find common ground for agreement among [the] parties without regard to preconceived ideas of our own about [a] final settlement. Only if [an] *impasse* is reached would we, as PCC member, wish to put forward terms of settlement, in which event we would consult with other members [of the] PCC as well as [the] British.[12]

Quest for an Advance Gesture from Israel

On the basis of the PCC's preliminary talks with Arab representatives, Ethridge concluded that the only way to make progress toward negotiations would be to obtain from the Israelis a conciliatory gesture regarding the return of refugees. In what was to become a dominant pattern of Israel-PCC-US relations, pressure for such an Israeli gesture would mount steadily, but would be met with an equally determined Israeli refusal. From these early discussions, it also became clear that the PCC and the Israelis would be adopting (and holding firm to) irreconcilable positions on the UN's call for the internationalization of Jerusalem. In its opposition to this international consensus regarding the Holy City, however, Israel had an important ally in Jordan, whose troops controlled the eastern part of the city.

Following its tour of Arab capitals, the commission returned to Israel for its official visit. The first of two high-level meetings took place on 24 February, the day of the signing of the Egyptian-Israel General Armistice Agreement (GAA) at Rhodes. Ethridge and his colleagues presented the two major Arab concerns as being (a) the return of the refugees, "but not necessarily" as a "condition precedent" for a final settlement, and (b) suspicions of Israel's general intentions. Foreign Minister Shertok pointed to the Rhodes signing to argue the case that concessions ought to be the result of direct Arab-Israeli negotiation, and not of Israel indicating possible concessions indirectly through third parties, such as the PCC.[13] This attitude would later become crystallized into Israel's critical and unwelcoming approach to UN conciliation and mediation generally.[14]

Regarding the substantive issues, the Israeli foreign minister went on to stress that two fundamental changes on the ground — "Arab aggression in Palestine" and the "exodus of Arab refugees" — had drastically altered the situation that had existed in late November 1947, when the UN partition resolution was adopted.

> [T]he Arab refugees who would be, hypothetically speaking, returning to Israel today would be returning to a totally different kind of country from the one in which they would have gone on living, had they never left.... We by no means take up the attitude that no Arab can ever return. We would be prepared to consider the return of a certain proportion, as part of the general peace settlement.

Shertok felt resettlement of these refugees "elsewhere" — rather than their repatriation to Israel — was essential. He affirmed that "Israel would be unable to consider repatriation." When pressed by Ethridge for an Israeli endorsement of the principles embodied in UNGA resolution 194, the foreign minister was evasive, except to restate Israel's rejection of the "abstract principle" that "as a matter of juridical right... anyone wishing to return must be allowed to return."[15]

Ethridge reported to Shertok and his aides that the PCC had found a "genuine desire for peace" during its tour of Arab capitals, but that the Arabs were "sincerely apprehensive *re* Israeli intentions." In what had already become a recurring theme of the PCC (and the US State Department) approach, he urged Israel to "find some way of indicating its concern" about the suffering of the refugees and to "demonstrate magnanimity" so that "Arab fears might be allayed and [a] new spirit might prevail which would permit progress." The commissioners informed the Israelis that they were tentatively considering holding a meeting with the Arab states to consider the refugee problem. A "conciliatory statement by Israel *re* refugees" at this time might, he suggested, facilitate progress towards a peace settlement. According to Ethridge's report to the secretary of state, Shertok was "impressed" by these arguments and "appreciated [the] importance of [a] conciliatory state[ment] in view [of] Arab psychology." The foreign minister reportedly promised to discuss the possibility of an "affirmative statement" with government officials. But the more detailed Israeli record of the meeting makes clear that Shertok raised several reservations about the utility of such a statement. He pointed to the direct Arab-Israeli contacts during the Rhodes talks "as proof as to what can effectively dissipate such fears."

The Israeli foreign minister also warned that, if his country were "drawn into making a statement" explicitly on the return of refugees as defined in the 11 December resolution, "it would have to be a negative statement."

A second meeting, involving Prime Minister David Ben-Gurion, took place the following morning. Again the PCC chairman conveyed the Arab view of the refugees as the main concern, which the commission felt

> constitute[d] such [a] human and psychological problem that if Israel could make [an] advance gesture regarding refugees, beyond concessions which might be made in negotiations, [a] general settlement would be greatly facilitated.

The commissioners again portrayed the Arab position as being one of wanting peace but fearing and distrusting Israel. The prime minister replied by stressing Israel's need for military security, which had to take precedence over its genuine desire for peace: "If we had not been capable of defending ourselves, they would have exterminated us without the world lifting a finger." Ethridge concluded the meeting by pointing out that "Arab distrust of Israeli intentions and Israeli insistence on military strength might both be resolved through deposit of negotiated treaties with [the] UN."[16]

CHAPTER 2

PCC Beirut Conference, March 1949

Following his round of shuttle diplomacy in various Middle Eastern capitals, Mark Ethridge summarized his main conclusions in two telegrams to Secretary of State Dean Acheson. He defined the refugee problem as the "immediate key to peace negotiations if not to peace." There could be no fruitful negotiation, however, "until the Arab psychosis as to [the] refugees has been wiped out and Arab public opinion prepared for [the] fact that not all refugees will return." The PCC chairman envisaged the first step towards peace negotiations as coming from Israel — viz., "some gesture of agreement in principle" with UNGA resolution 194's clauses regarding the refugees. He had sought from Shertok, and felt sure he would soon obtain, such an "action or statement," which would then allow the commission "entry to other problems" during the forthcoming meeting with the Arab states. Reflecting the view, held by all parties, that representations from the US State Department had played an important role in persuading the Egyptians and Israelis to overcome their differences and sign the GAA, Ethridge also attributed a recent improvement in Shertok's and Ben-Gurion's attitude (compared with the commission's first visit in early February) to a "stiffened American attitude" and the "moves" which the State Department had made "to indicate to the Israeli government that it wants peace here." The US representative on the PCC, therefore, sought to enlist his government's help in encouraging the appropriate Israeli and Arab behavior in the form of obtaining a conciliatory Israeli gesture on the return of Palestinian refugees, and a favorable Arab response once that gesture were made.[1]

Ethridge confirmed the commission's plans to convene a meeting with Arab representatives, to be followed by an attempt at Arab-Israeli negotiation. The scheduled PCC conference of all the invited Arab representatives meeting together in Beirut would establish an important precedent in terms of the structure of the conciliation talks. Israel's serious misgivings about the PCC's stress on the gesture required of them were matched by an equally serious concern regarding the proposed structure of the commission's scheduled conference with the Arabs.

The contrast to Rhodes was striking. Almost a month before the Beirut meetings, Moshe Shertok had advised Ethridge against meeting with the various Arab representatives *en bloc.* "I foresee a certain danger there," he warned the PCC in late February.

> This may result in their entrenching themselves behind a certain line from which it will perhaps be very difficult for them to retreat, seeing that it has been a line commonly agreed upon.

Political courage in the Arab world, he advised, was "in inverse ratio to the number of people present."[2] There were others, including the British ambassador to Iraq, who had also counseled the commission against trying to meet all the Arab states in one conference.[3] On the eve of the scheduled Beirut conference, the attitude and behavior of the PCC worried Eliahu Sasson to the point of wondering whether "its members [were] postponing peace instead of bringing it nearer." Relying not only on his own extensive experience of talks with Arab representatives, but citing also the views of a member of the Egyptian delegation at Rhodes, Sasson complained that, in the proposed format, "the participants incite one another to intransigence and xenophobia." He hoped that American policy makers could be persuaded to "get the Commission to... follow the methods of Dr. Bunche and invite each Arab State separately to negotiate with Israel."[4]

But avoidance of finding themselves in such a one-on-one bargaining situation was precisely what motivated most Arab leaders (with the notable exceptions of King Abdallah and his prime minister, Tawfiq Abu al-Huda)[5] at this time. During the PCC's preliminary tour of Arab capitals, a number of efforts had been made to coordinate the policies of the various states on the Palestine question.[6] British strategic interest in maintaining secure land communication for its troops throughout the region expressed itself, especially during January and February 1949, in concern that Egypt and Jordan should coordinate their sometimes conflicting approaches to the Palestine issue and their claims to the Negev.[7] In the weeks leading up to the PCC Beirut conference, Prime Minister Nuri Sa'id had his own reasons for appealing to Egypt in the quest for a unified Arab stance *vis-à-vis* the commission. According to the Iraqi chief of staff, Nuri was proposing a united Arab front which would press the PCC to endorse the demand for the return of the refugees without conditions or limitation, along with a recognition of the city of Jerusalem as Arab. Once the Israelis submitted their own far-reaching claims and rejected these key Arab demands, Nuri hoped that Israel's intransigence on political issues, as well as its refusal to return to the October 1948 cease-fire lines, would lead to a US-Israeli rift, accompanied by a strict arms embargo on the Jewish state. During this time, he hoped, Iraq and the Arabs would be rearmed with British assistance while the US and UK would be drawn away from supporting the Jews to backing the Arabs.[8]

On 1 March 1949, invitations went out to the foreign ministers of the seven Arab League states to meet in three weeks' time with the PCC in Beirut. On 17 March, the Arab League Council adopted a resolution demanding the right of Palestinian refugees to return to their homes, and recommending that Arab representatives "consult together... before meeting the Conciliation Commission in Beirut on 21 March."[9] In preparing for its Beirut meeting with high-ranking representatives of the Arab states, the PCC strove for Arab agreement to discussions that would go beyond the refugee issue. During the February tour, the commission had tried to convince Arab officials of the "utter unrealism" of their original position which had insisted on a satisfactory resolution of the refugee issue before proceeding to discuss any other issues. The commission saw among its current tasks the need to "make [the Arabs] realize: (a) That not all refugees will go back, (b) That they must help find homes for those to be resettled outside Israel." The Beirut meetings were also seen as a delicate step towards Arab-Israeli negotiation, one which would also be dependent on the Israelis' acceptance in principle of UNGA resolution 194 on refugees.[10]

British diplomats in the Middle East joined their American counterparts in urging Arab leaders to attend the conference and to adopt a constructive attitude.[11] The Syrian prime minister informed the American minister in Damascus that, despite the pressure of "public opinion" on the Palestine issue, he recognized that,

> as part of the price of effective western friendship, concessions must be made and [a] settlement reached.... Hoping that [the] PCC will be [the] means of assuring [the] Arabs [a] fair settlement, Syria [was] prepared to cooperate with it in good faith.

In a similar discussion with Syrian President Shukri al-Quwatli, the US minister, James Keeley, made it quite explicit that a favorable American attitude to foreign aid to Syria might be linked with progress toward a Palestine settlement.[12]

But a week before the scheduled opening of the conference, Ethridge reported to the State Department that the commission's work in Beirut was being "seriously prejudiced" by recent Israeli statements and military actions (Operation "Uvda," for the conquest of the Negev to the Gulf of Aqaba), but especially by the continued "failure or refusal of [the] Israeli Government to make any statement re refugees that would put [the] Commission in [a] position to find a key for peace negotiations." The PCC was so worried about the likelihood of failure that it had even considered canceling the conference. But before giving in to despair, Ethridge asked whether the State Department could "do anything useful during Shertok's visit" to the US "to induce him to make one conciliatory gesture." Because, in Ethridge's view, the Israeli leader "consider[ed] Washington more friendly than the Commission" and had "not been sufficiently impressed with US interest in [a] UN settlement," the PCC representative ended his cable with the hope that Shertok "could be shown that this is not the case." Ethridge pointed to growing Arab cynicism regarding the UN and the consequent need to consider US or joint Anglo-American "guarantees" for any projected settlement.[13]

On 21 March 1949, the PCC convened with Arab foreign ministers and representatives of Palestinian refugee groups at the St. George's Hotel in Beirut. Mark Ethridge summarized the Israeli position, as he had understood it from his talks with Ben-Gurion and Shertok, and invited the ministers' responses. Ahmad Shuqayri, who attended the meeting as an aide to Syrian Prime Minister Khalid al-Azm, recalled that the ministers "explained the right of the refugees to return to their homeland as being a natural right" and "spoke at length about the Palestine question with emphasis on [their] rejection of the partition resolution and [their] non-recognition of all that derived from it." Shuqayri himself took the floor to complain about the Israeli government's lack of commitment to UNGA resolution 194 which spoke of the return of refugees. "With regard to the refugees," Shuqayri added,

> there is a clause in the resolution which urges [them] to live in peace with "their neighbors." The neighbors are one thing, and the government of Israel is another. Everyone laughed [he recalled] at the legal play on words!

Reflecting back on the tactics used by the Arab states during these Beirut meetings, Shuqayri wrote:

> In fact, the subject of the refugees was the core of the tactics between ourselves and Israel.... This logic was simple and plain. It needed execution, except that the keys to the country were in Israel's hands. She was playing unfairly and deceptively; she tied the subject of the refugees to the Palestine issue as a whole. It was absolutely out of the question that the Palestine issue, the how and when, be resolved, as I stated before the Conciliation Commission on that day, so long as Israel wanted to tie the subject of the refugees with the Rock of Mount Tariq.... She would not be moved unless the mountain moved.[14]

Following the 21 March session with Arab foreign ministers, the PCC met to consider its next steps, which included the need to impress upon the Arabs that it was "doubtful" whether Israel would be able to absorb "more than a small number of refugees" and that the Arab states should prepare themselves to "attempt [to] resettle refugees and initiate projects for absorbing them."[15] The commission also recommended the start of peace talks, especially on a territorial settlement, as soon as possible after the Beirut conference and the armistice talks being held in Rhodes. Finally, reflecting the "increasing conviction . . . that economic development [was the] key to [a] long-range solution [to the] refugee problem," the PCC recommended the setting up of a "committee of experts to survey [the] economic needs of the area" in connection with the reintegration of Palestinian refugees.[16]

At the close of the Beirut conference, the PCC informed the Arabs that it had found the discussions useful, but that a proper study of the problems involved would "necessitate continuous meetings with the two parties in a neutral place." Egypt, Jordan, Syria and Lebanon indicated their readiness to attend such meetings once the commission made clear that no direct Israeli-Arab meetings were contemplated.[17] Iraq refused to attend. After overcoming some resistance from the UN secretary general,[18] the PCC went ahead with plans to convene talks with Arabs and Israelis in Lausanne, Switzerland.

CHAPTER 3

Towards Lausanne: Continuing Pressure for an Israeli Gesture

One of the conclusions reached by the PCC after its Beirut meetings was that the "maximum possible repatriation" of refugees to Israel was a "necessary precedent to any satisfactory solution [of the] refugee population through resettlement." The representatives of the Arab states had "consistently refused [to] consider resettlement until satisfactory action [was] taken [on] repatriation." For their part, representatives of the refugee groups "expressed [their] unanimous desire [to] return to [their] homes" in accordance with the UN resolution, and "express[ed] confidence they [could] live at peace with the Jews." Believing that they had succeeded in coming away from Beirut with "a real concession" in the form of Arab "agreement to go ahead with peace talks" (despite unpropitious circumstances), the commission was now, more anxiously than before, looking for the Israeli gesture on refugees that would help assure a successful start for the proposed talks.[1]

The quest for such a gesture — undertaken even while Ethridge appreciated that the refugees had become, for the Arab states, "a political weapon against the Jews"[2] — was advanced on two fronts simultaneously: Secretary of State Acheson in the US and members of the PCC in Israel. Contrary to the views of some contemporary observers and retrospective scholars alike,[3] the US State Department became increasingly mobilized in the commission's efforts to put pressure on the Israeli authorities. On 5 April, Dean Acheson met in New York for talks with Foreign Minister Sharett (who had recently hebraized his name from Shertok). The secretary was as forceful as he could have been on behalf of the PCC, but fell short of hinting at any actual American sanctions. Invoking directly the views of President Truman throughout the conversation, Acheson's phraseology overtly stressed a "carrot," but contained a "stick" between the lines:

> a statesmanlike move by Israel with respect to refugees would make it possible for the President to continue his strong and warm support for Israel and efforts being made by its Government to establish its new political and economic structure on a firm basis.

Acheson also noted that the President was

> particularly anxious that an *impasse* not develop on this subject, with one side refusing to negotiate for a final settlement until a solution is found for refugees, and the other side refusing to take steps to solve the refugee question until there is a final political settlement. We must avoid the argument as to which is the horse and which is the cart.

The secretary even advanced concrete suggestions regarding a proposed announcement by Israel about its readiness to repatriate "a portion, say a fourth, of the refugees eligible for repatriation," and outlined a possible timetable for the phased implementation of repatriation, to go hand-in-hand with progress in talks about a political settlement. But the Israeli foreign minister replied by restating the well-known Israeli position "that the refugee problem [could] only be solved in terms of [a] final peace settlement and that basically resettlement [was] the proper solution for [the] refugees." While appreciating the American concern for breaking the "vicious circle" between repatriation and a final peace settlement, Sharett remained opposed to any "pre-peace commitment" on repatriation of specific numbers.[4]

Following the Acheson-Sharett conversation, the commission's scheduled meeting with Prime Minister Ben-Gurion on 7 April took on all the makings of a showdown. During the two-and-a-half-hour session, "no punches [were] pulled [on] either side." On the issue of Jerusalem, there was no meeting of minds but rather — in the words of the director-general of Israel's foreign ministry, Dr. Walter Eytan,

— an "agreement to differ."[5] After discussing ideas for a series of meetings in a neutral city, PCC Chairman Yalçin went to the heart of the issue by repeating the commission's long-standing request for Israel to accept the "principle of repatriation, resettlement and rehabilitation" as laid down in UNGA resolution 194 of 11 December 1948. Ben-Gurion's reply dwelt on the phrase in paragraph 11 of that resolution about "those refugees wishing to return to their homes and live at peace with their neighbors." In the Israeli view, as long as peace had not yet been achieved, and since "it was not yet clear [that the] Arabs wished to live at peace," the implementation of this resolution would "depend on whether peaceful relations were established between Israel and [the] Arab states."[6]

Yalçin then appealed to Israel not to deny basic human rights to the "Arab people" for possible wrongs committed by the "Arab states." He warned that "world sympathy which had assisted [the] Jews in reaching [the] promised land" would be "alienated" if Israel, "like Hitler, use[d] methods incompatible with standards of western civilization." In reply, Ben-Gurion spoke "with considerable emotion" of the refugee issue as being "an organized plan by [the] Arab states or [the] British or both." He repeated that resettlement of the Arabs in Arab states would be "more humane than in Israel," and pledged that Israel "would not forget [the] humanitarian side of [the] question" once these issues were raised as part of a peace settlement.

At this point the American representative, Mark Ethridge, joined the 7 April discussions, pointing to the "great concession" the Arabs had made to the commission by backing down from their previous "unrealistic" position of not wishing to discuss anything until the refugee problem had been satisfactorily settled. Again he appealed to Israel to make a "conciliatory gesture" which was the "key" to a solution. An Israeli gesture, Ethridge argued, would be appreciated not only by the Arab states, but also by the US government, the American people and world opinion, which was growing increasingly critical of the Israeli role in the flight of Arabs from their homes and lands. Ben-Gurion (apparently not agreeing with Secretary Acheson's views on the "horse-and-cart" logic) affirmed that "the key to peace in

Palestine [was] not a solution to the refugee problem, but vice versa: the key to solving the refugee problem [was] peace." The Israeli prime minister remained firm in refusing to make such a move prior to a peace settlement, adding that the re-introduction of large numbers of Arabs into his "small" country would create a potential fifth column. As much as Israel valued international opinion, "self-preservation" was more important than world sympathy; Israel was prepared, if necessary, to "contradict [the] PCC which represented great individual states and [the] UN."

The PCC continued to press Israeli leaders for the advance gesture on refugee repatriation. Several days later, it addressed a memorandum to the government of Israel, formally suggesting that Israel "might well" undertake several "preliminary measures... for the purpose of creating an atmosphere favorable to the success of the forthcoming exchanges of views" at Lausanne. The list of seven "confidence-building" measures began with a request for a general declaration that the government of Israel would "cooperate to the fullest possible extent in the solution of the refugee problem," and was followed by six specific assurances regarding absentee property rights, treatment of the Arab minority, etc. Weeks later, Ethridge would still be complaining of his disappointment at Israel's failure to provide a satisfactory reply to this memorandum.[7]

After delivery of his 11 April memorandum, Ethridge wrote personally to President Truman, offering a frank assessment of Arab and Israeli positions and the prevailing mood he encountered in both camps. As Ethridge described it, the Arabs had made "what the Commission consider[ed] very great concessions," while the Jews had "made none so far." He was appreciative of Truman's previous support, and hoped the president could "keep the pressure up."[8] Yet, after a wide-ranging talk with Michael Comay of the Israel Foreign Ministry, Ethridge reported dejectedly that, in spite of all the State Department had done since January, Israel had "stiffened rather than modified her position," taking advantage of every Arab weakness and producing armistice agreements based on "unfair arrangements" that would have "serious repercussions in [the] Middle East and tend to discredit" the US and the UN.[9]

On 18 April, Ethridge was invited to an informal meeting with the Israeli prime minister in the resort town of Tiberias. The American PCC representative responded to Ben-Gurion's initiative under the impression that the discussion would be about the long-sought conciliatory statement on the refugee question. As the conversation progressed, however, Ethridge waited in vain for Ben-Gurion to commit himself to making a public statement, and heard instead only a repetition of the basic Israeli positions on Jerusalem, territory and refugees. Regarding the latter, the prime minister emphasized resettlement, and spoke of the possible reunion of separated families, compensation, etc. During the following months, Ethridge would frequently single out this conversation with varying degrees of bitterness and anger, at one point suggesting that Israel had "lost [the] peace" by ignoring his memorandum of 11 April and by Ben-Gurion's attitude at Tiberias.[10]

As the date for the Lausanne conference approached, the cumulative criticisms by the PCC, the US and Britain of the Israeli attitude to the refugee question found their way into the Arabic press.[11] Meanwhile, Washington's disappointment in Israeli "intransigence," as evidenced in Ben-Gurion's last conversation with Ethridge, became linked with the question of the imminent UN vote on Israel's admission to that body. While Israelis were hoping to complete the UN debates over admission before beginning the Lausanne discussions, both Ethridge and the American consul general in Jerusalem recommended the postponement of the admission question as a form of pressure on Israel.[12]

But rather than pushing for a delay of the debates, the State Department decided that the degree of active American support for Israel's membership would be conditional upon a cooperative attitude towards the PCC and the forthcoming Lausanne conference. A stern warning was drafted in the State Department on 20 April (but was not sent).[13] In a meeting with Israel's Ambassador Elath in Washington and UN representative Eban, Secretary of State Acheson reviewed American disappointment at the continuing lack of moderation in

Sharett's and Ben-Gurion's positions. While disclaiming any intention of "trying to tell the Israeli government what it should do," Acheson made it plain that the US "had supported Israel's application for membership and would continue to do so" — but it would be "difficult for the US delegation to go to the other nations at Lake Success and endeavor to persuade them they should also vote for Israel's admission this session" unless the Israeli government was "willing to make its position known" on the important issues of refugees, Jerusalem, and territorial adjustments.[14]

But the threat of receiving only lukewarm American support at the UN was not sufficient to produce any far-reaching conciliatory statements in time for the opening of the Lausanne talks. In fact, the Israelis undertook a counteroffensive in New York on the admission question, arguing that the lack of US "active interest" in the "earliest" resolution of the issue at the UN would lead to "inevitable difficulties [at] Lausanne" and would "increase Arab unwillingness [to] conclude peace [with] Israel." The Israeli argument seems to have had at least some effect.[15]

"After nine weeks," Ethridge reported proudly (if not altogether accurately) on 19 April, "we have persuaded [the] Arabs to sit down for peace talks with the Jews."[16] But the American PCC representative remained frustrated at not having obtained the desired gesture from Israel. American pressure for a conciliatory gesture continued and even increased, but seems not to have had a serious impact upon Israeli preparations for Lausanne. At the same time, Secretary Acheson instructed American envoys in the Arab world to make the "strongest diplomatic approach" to prime ministers and foreign ministers in an "endeavor to soften their... attitudes... and to support [the] PCC in its task" at Lausanne. The British Foreign Office was being asked to make similar approaches to Arab governments.[17]

The Shadow of Rhodes

In the weeks leading up to the Lausanne conference, both Israelis and Arabs drew upon the lessons of the Rhodes experience. In our own day, one of the criticisms leveled at the PCC by Israeli analysts is that "it did not emulate Dr. Bunche's successful technique of organizing face-to-face meetings under UN auspices."[18] Indeed, this would become a frequent refrain in the growing Israeli critique of the commission during and after 1949.

During his meeting with the PCC on 24 February, Foreign Minister Sharett had developed at length Israel's arguments for preferring direct negotiations to third-party conciliation. The success of the talks at Rhodes was, he claimed, "to be ascribed directly to the fact that they were direct negotiations between two parties." While paying "high tribute to the part played by the Mediator and his advisers," Sharett argued that the success was largely due to the fact that the parties had been brought together and allowed to confront each other over concrete issues, leading to a "process of give and take."[19]

Israeli preparations for the Lausanne conference reflected, in the words of one Israeli scholar, "a mood anticipating threats and pressures rather than a welcome breakthrough."[20] During the first of several daylong strategy sessions devoted to the forthcoming talks, the Israeli prime minister stressed the centrality of immigration and security to Israel's future, and placed the need for peace with the Arabs in this context. This obliged Israel to "spare no effort in achieving peace." A further advantage was that peace with the Arabs would reduce the interference of foreign powers in Middle Eastern affairs. Tactically, Ben-Gurion suggested that Israel strive for direct and separate negotiations with each Arab state, if possible without the knowledge of the others.[21] In addition, Israel hoped to replicate the Rhodes experience with opportunities for direct, informal contacts outside the framework of official meetings under UN auspices.[22]

But Israel was virtually alone in hoping that the precedent of direct negotiations with individual Arab states at Rhodes would provide a model which the PCC would follow in setting up forthcoming

Arab-Israeli discussions in Lausanne. Only Jordan's King Abdallah seemed to share this view. On 3 April, Jordan and Israel signed a GAA at Rhodes, although the terms had been worked out in secret talks between Israeli representatives and Abdallah at Shuneh.[23] Ten days later, the king declared to the American *chargé d'affaires* in Amman that "any meeting in which all Arab states took part would not result in progress toward peace."[24]

But the bilateral Rhodes experience could not simply be imitated or replicated at Lausanne, which was necessarily a multilateral event. For the same reasons that Israelis had come to look on the Rhodes model as the one to be followed at Lausanne, most of the Arab states had rejected the "island of shame"[25] when it was first suggested as a possible venue for PCC talks. The humiliation of defeat symbolized by Rhodes would constitute, for the Arab side, one of the obstacles to progress at Lausanne. The Arab governments had not adequately prepared their people for the true nature or extent of the military setbacks which their armies had suffered in the battle for Palestine.

As the date of the Lausanne talks approached, the Arab public was just beginning to realize that their leaders had signed armistice agreements in which they were not the victors, but the vanquished.[26] In this atmosphere Arab spokesmen dared not admit openly that they had agreed to attend a "peace conference" with the Israeli enemy — worse still, an enemy which was defying with impunity the UN resolution calling for the return of the refugees. On the eve of the opening of the conference, an Arab League spokesman described the Lausanne talks as merely a continuation of the Beirut meetings, with the refugee problem as the major issue on the agenda.[27]

Strains in the Arab Common Front

Below the surface, the invitations to attend the conference at Lausanne put a strain on the common front which the Arab states may have hoped to maintain. Iraq simply refused to attend. The British ambassador in Baghdad reported that the Iraqis were "using [the] refugee question as an excuse and say that they will not negotiate until [the] refugees return to their homes."[28] King Abdallah of Jordan, anxious to preserve his freedom of maneuver, outlined his plans to send a delegation to Lausanne in a conversation with the American *chargé d'affaires* in Amman, but indicated that a peace settlement between his country and Israel "would be reached in direct talks held in this area."[29] Following a secret meeting with senior Israeli officials at the king's Shuneh palace on 15 April, Abdallah became even more committed to the idea of a separate peace with Israel, with or without approval of the other Arab states; but the Jordanian monarch did want such an arrangement to be guaranteed by either the PCC or one or more of the Western powers.[30] Ethridge and other observers saw Abdallah as "so anxious" to deal directly with Israel that they felt it necessary to caution him against going too far, fearing that his independent action would provoke sharper opposition among Palestinians and the other Arab states, thereby jeopardizing PCC efforts at Lausanne.[31]

Despite the clear signals which Abdallah sent secretly to British, American and Israeli officials, his public stance called for the joining of forces of Arab delegations in solidarity at the Lausanne conference. This declared position was in harmony with contemporary newspaper editorials warning against allowing separate negotiations like the ones from which Israel had benefited at Rhodes.[32] Notwithstanding such public statements, there was a "growing conviction" in Jerusalem that the Jordanian delegation to Lausanne would become, like its counterpart at Rhodes, "mainly a cloak for negotiations at Shuneh"[33] — i.e., between Abdallah and the Israelis. Foreign Minister Sharett himself met with the Jordanian monarch on 5 May.[34] Indeed, the existence of this separate track of secret bilateral Israeli-Jordan talks would necessarily result in both the Israeli and Jordanian delegations at Lausanne devoting less serious attention to the multilateral conference organized by the PCC.

In the end, the representatives of four states and a handful of Palestinian refugee organizations prepared to attend the Lausanne conference. This multiplicity of Arab actors, encompassing potentially divergent grievances, interests and policies, threatened to create complications for both the Arabs and the conference organizers. This issue would be partly resolved during the first week of the talks, when the PCC would agree to deal with the various Arab delegations as a single group (see below). Both inside and outside of the formal sessions, the Egyptians, Syrians and Lebanese did their best to ensure that "Jordan in Lausanne" behaved better than "Jordan in Amman."[35]

Another issue, of minor importance to the invited participants at the time, was the question of Palestinian representation. Some behind-the-scenes maneuvering took place in Amman regarding inclusion of a Palestinian in the Jordanian delegation to Lausanne.[36] The most visible Palestinian presence at the conference was to come, however, from outside the Jordanian delegation. Muhammad Nimr al-Hawwari and Aziz Shihadeh, heads of the General Refugee Congress based in Ramallah, would spend most of their time and energy in a frustrating struggle for acceptance and credibility on three fronts: to be formally received by the PCC, to coordinate strategy with the Arab delegations, and to persuade the Israelis to recognize their delegation and deal directly with it towards an acceptable solution. Hawwari's credentials were not accepted by the Arab delegations, and at one point representatives from the All-Palestine Government based in Gaza visited Lausanne in order to discredit him. The Israelis, while pleased to maintain regular contacts with the refugee delegation, did not wish to negotiate with it officially, and attempted in vain to enlist Hawwari's people in the quest for direct negotiations between Israel and the Arab governments.[37] Years later, one Palestinian writer would refer to Eliahu Sasson's talks with Hawwari and with representatives of the Arab states as illustrating the "mindset" of the Zionists and their attempts to "eliminate the national rights of the Palestinian people under the guise of a 'peaceful solution to the Palestine question'."[38]

Adding to the confusion was another Palestinian, Ahmad Khalil, then serving as military governor of the northern area of the West Bank, who attempted to win British, American and Israeli support for a peace settlement based on the partition boundaries, annexation of Arab Palestine to Transjordan, and the implementation of the UNGA resolution 194 on refugees. He claimed to have Abdallah's blessing for his efforts and, on the eve of the Lausanne talks, signaled to Israelis in Jerusalem that a three-man Palestinian delegation in Switzerland would "try and enter into direct negotiations with Israel, as was favored," he claimed, "by many of the local inhabitants."[39]

CHAPTER 4

Opening the Conference

Maneuvering for Position

While the PCC, Arabs and Israelis were preparing to attend the Lausanne meetings, the State Department's George McGhee was given responsibility for studying the practical implications of economic development and refugee resettlement. In anticipation of a political breakthrough in the coming Arab-Israeli negotiations, British and American experts stepped up their work on a "plan of operations" for resolving the refugee problem, plans which would eventually lead to the creation of an "Economic Survey Mission" (ESM).[1]

The first Lausanne meeting between the Israeli delegation and the PCC took place at the Hotel Beau Rivage on 27 April 1949. It was a straightforward affair which covered familiar ground. Israeli delegate Gershon Hirsch (later Avner) described it as beginning with heartfelt greetings and Ethridge's renewed request for a declaration of Israel's stand on refugees, Jerusalem and boundaries. On the major issues, Hirsch's reply contained nothing the commissioners had not heard before. The Israeli delegation also expressed its hope that the proceedings for Israel's admission to the UN would not be allowed to interfere with the progress of the current talks; in fact, fearful that members of the PCC might attempt to influence the UN debates on Israel's admission to the UN, Ambassador Eban recommended to Israelis at Lausanne that they indicate to the commissioners the "impropriety" of such activity.[2] The Israeli delegation also declared that it was not willing to negotiate with Syria at Lausanne until after the signing of an armistice agreement between the two countries.[3]

On 30 April, Walter Eytan, who arrived to head the Israeli delegation, met the press and distributed a government *communiqué* which expressed Israel's determination to do everything possible "towards the attainment of an honorable and lasting peace under the auspices of the United Nations Conciliation Commission and by direct contact with the delegations of the Arab states." Israel looked forward to a permanent settlement and to the "rehabilitation of all those who left their homes in the course of armed attacks against Israel." Privately, however, Eytan was critical that a vague statement such as this would be "interpreted by everyone as yet another attempt by us to shirk the real issues."[4]

Earlier recriminations between Mark Ethridge and Israeli representatives spilled over into the first weeks at Lausanne. In formal and informal meetings, the commissioners repeatedly requested an Israeli reply to the PCC memorandum of 11 April as a conciliatory statement on repatriation necessary for progress in the talks. Ethridge grew impatient upon noticing no change in the Israeli stand as originally outlined to him by Ben-Gurion. He was especially disappointed that several weeks of pressure from Washington had "apparently fallen on deaf ears."[5]

During the PCC's first sessions with the Egyptian and Lebanese delegations, the latter offered expressions of their willingness to cooperate with the commission and their desire for peace; but the PCC's horse-and-cart dilemma still remained, as the Arabs insisted that a solution to the refugee problem and Jerusalem was "essential before peace talks could progress."[6] Public statements from Arab delegates downplayed the "peace conference" aspect of the meetings, stressing instead their function as PCC efforts at resolving the refugee problem and the Jerusalem issue and noting that there would be no direct contacts with the Israeli delegation.[7] Walter Eytan noticed that the Arabs, continuing the stance adopted during the previous months, "seem to have agreed among themselves to talk refugees and nothing else."[8] In a private conversation with Mark Ethridge, however, Jordanian delegate Fawzi al-Mulqi indicated "in no uncertain terms" that his government considered the achievement of a "quick peace" to be the primary objective of the meetings. Signals like these made Ethridge even more upset with the Israelis, who, he felt,

> apparently fail to appreciate [the] importance of [a] conciliatory approach toward outstanding problems. Arab fears re public opinion at home are deprecated. Maximum concessions from [the] Arabs appear to be more important to [the] Israelis than [a] constructive conclusion to [the] recent conflict.[9]

After one week of formal opening sessions and private conversations, the commissioners reported their underlying impression that both sides were "sincerely desirous of making peace arrangements" as soon as possible, but were "maneuvering for position." In particular, discussions were stalled because the question of Israel's admission to the UN was "overshadowing everything else," and also because Ethridge was awaiting word from the State Department and the president on an outline of the McGhee plan for refugee resettlement. The Arabs realized that they had the Israelis "on the carpet," and indicated to Ethridge that they were unwilling to start talking "until the struggle at the UN ha[d] been fought to the finish." Privately, Ethridge appeared not unhappy at this situation, which he hoped would lead to the Israelis receiving a "bloody nose" over the admission question and might put them "into a more reasonable frame of mind meanwhile." The commissioners did not hide from Walter Eytan their feelings that the Israelis had "so far treated them cavalierly and done very little to help them in their task."[10]

On 4 May 1949, Abba (Aubrey) Eban issued a statement at the United Nations on the refugee question. The seven-point statement began by declaring that the refugee problem was one for which the Arab states were "entirely responsible;" Israel was nevertheless

> anxious to contribute to the solution of this problem, although it is none of its making. This anxiety proceeds from moral considerations and from Israel's vital interest in stable conditions throughout the Near East.

After weighing the advantages and disadvantages of rehabilitating the refugees in Israel or in the neighboring countries, the government of Israel "contend[ed] that resettlement in neighboring areas be considered the main principle of solution." Israel was "ready to make its own contribution to the solution of the problem," but the extent of that contribution would, "*inter alia*, depend on the formal establishment of peace and relations of good neighborliness between Israel and the Arab States." Absent from the statement was any Israeli commitment (or reference) to "repatriation." The statement appealed to "the States which caused the problem by their initiative in proclaiming war last year" to "face squarely their responsibilities," and ended by noting that "an immediate declaration by all Governments of their desire for an early peace settlement would create a favorable atmosphere for discussion of this problem."[11]

Although the tone and contents of such a declaration could hardly have been viewed by the Arabs as a conciliatory gesture, Eytan forwarded this statement to Ethridge at Lausanne with a covering note describing it as "an earnest attempt to meet the views of the United States Government on the solution to the refugee problem." Ambassador Elath conveyed the same message to the State Department.[12] The French member of the PCC, Claude de Boisanger, found Eytan's statements on compensation "wholly unsatisfactory and in complete contradiction with the terms of the [UN December 1948] resolution."[13] Two days later, Eytan provided a supplementary statement making specific reference to points raised in the PCC memorandum of 11 April, in an attempt to go further towards creating an atmosphere favorable to the success of the conference. The PCC replied on 18 May, requesting reconsideration of several items.[14]

It was not until the second week in May that some movement in Lausanne was possible, overcoming the delays and hesitations surrounding the US-Israeli tug-of-war regarding the gesture on refugees and Israel's admission into the UN. Finally, when Israel was admitted to membership in the United Nations on 11 May 1949, Ambassador Elath wrote a letter of gratitude to Secretary Acheson. The letter was conciliatory in tone, spoke optimistically about the prospect of progress at Lausanne, but did not deny the persistence of differences between Israel and the UNGA on several crucial issues.[15] From Lausanne, Ethridge was "glad to report" that, despite his earlier fears, the Israeli delegates' attitude had "not seemed to change for the worse" following admission to the United Nations. The PCC representative did, however, note renewed expressions of Arab mistrust of American policies and cynicism regarding America's willingness or ability to obtain assurances regarding Israeli adherence to UN resolutions.[16] One potential improvement in the atmosphere at Lausanne was the reported instruction of the Egyptian government to its delegation: "since Israel [is] now [a] member [of the] UN, if she accepts [the] principle of [the] right of refugees to return, you are authorized [to] discuss [a] territorial settlement."[17] But this potential was to go unfulfilled.

Structures and Procedures

During the opening weeks at Lausanne, structures and procedures were established which came to constitute a distinctive Lausanne format for PCC peacemaking efforts, notably a series of parallel PCC-Arab and PCC-Israel meetings, with no *official, direct* Arab-Israeli meetings. For this reason, some have taken to placing quotation marks around the word "conference,"[18] as others have done in the case of the similarly-structured St. James's Palace "round table conference" convened by the British in February-March 1939. Yet the Lausanne discussions do qualify as a conference within the definition proposed by international relations specialists.[19]

1. *Two-track PCC operations.* The commissioners continued their practice of alternating formal meetings with informal conversations involving individual members of the commission and members of the various delegations.

2. *Indirect negotiation at the official level.* Although not in principle opposed to direct Arab-Israeli meetings at the conference, the PCC kept its word to the Arab delegates that they would not be expected to

hold face-to-face meetings with their Israeli counterparts. During its first official meeting with the Israel delegation, the PCC announced that it intended to meet separately with Arab and Israeli delegations, but that it would be ready to assist Israeli and Arab delegates to meet each other, with or without its participation.[20] Mark Ethridge was quoted in the Hebrew press as saying:

> I am sure that before the end of the conference direct negotiations will take place between them, but in the meantime both sides are not distancing themselves from the blood and the bitterness, and some time will pass before the heat subsides in them.[21]

But the PCC never tried to force Arabs and Israelis to meet around the same table — a fact which later became the centerpiece of the Israeli critique of UN mediation efforts.

3. *Direct, secret and informal Arab-Israeli contacts.* As one scholar has pointed out, "one of the few positive results of this singularly futile international conference was the cover it provided for direct contacts between the principal protagonists themselves."[22] Unofficial, direct Arab-Israeli contacts took late place on at least twenty occasions over the course of the entire Lausanne conference, outside its formal framework.[23] As far as Israel was concerned, such informal contacts proved more valuable than the formal conference; yet, they were no substitute for the direct talks which it persistently demanded between the delegations on the official level. Some of the unofficial meetings took place with the knowledge of either the commissioners, or the various delegations, or both. But they were not as easy to arrange as they had been at Rhodes. During the latter conference, all delegations had been housed in the same hotel; in Lausanne, Israeli delegates stayed at the same hotel with the PCC, while the Arab delegations were installed in another part of town.[24]

Given the state of public opinion in the Arab countries, the conference served as a necessary fig leaf to cover such secret contacts. These informal and unofficial meetings were appreciated by both Israelis and Arabs — not because they led to any breakthrough, but because they enabled the parties to probe for any prospect of compromise behind the inevitable hard-line posturing by the delegations before the PCC. They were not, however, endorsed by the US State Department, which looked on them as a factor undermining rather than enhancing the effectiveness of the main efforts of the PCC towards a comprehensive settlement.[25] Despite several hopeful reports indicating possibilities for agreement on bilateral issues, the overall weight of the available evidence does not support one scholar's recent description of these secret dialogues as being "characterized by great flexibility on the part of all concerned."[26] It would be far more accurate to say that these probings only confirmed the existence of a wide gap between the positions of Arabs and Israelis and provided no real opportunities to bridge that gap.

4. *Arab representation: a single delegation.* After initially holding separate meetings with the Egyptian and Lebanese delegations, the PCC was confronted with the Arab delegations' joint "decision in principle to negotiate with the commission only *en bloc.*" Although French representative Claude de Boisanger considered this a "dangerous precedent," the PCC soon acquiesced in the Arab demand. To the chagrin of the Israelis, the pattern established for the remainder of the Lausanne conference was for the Arab delegations to negotiate with the PCC only *en bloc.*[27]

5. *No PCC proposals for a settlement.* One of the recurring dynamics of the Lausanne conference was the push and pull between the PCC and the Arab delegations over where the initiative lay for outlining the possible terms of a solution. The commissioners declined the Arab delegations' request on 5 May for "a working paper presenting the complete outline of a settlement," and attempted instead to elicit further position papers from the Arabs on issues other than the refugee question. The line which was to be followed fairly consistently by the PCC — and one which corresponded to the US State Department and Israeli positions on this issue — was for the commission not to submit its own proposals for a settlement "unless the positions taken up by the Arab and Israeli delegations proved irreconcilable."[28]

In throwing the ball back into the Arabs' court, Ethridge was conscious of the tactical maneuvering of some Arab delegates who

> want[ed] to be in a position to say that peace was imposed by [the] UN. In fact, two of them have told me that if I will draft a peace plan they will consider it as [an] 'instruction.' I have of course refused to do so both on behalf of the US and [the] UN.[29]

The only real exception to this rule of PCC non-intervention was the submission to the parties of a declaration of principles soon to be known as the Lausanne Protocol.

CHAPTER 5

A Basis for Discussion: The Lausanne Protocol, 12 May 1949

By early May, the commission had received a number of Israeli statements and position papers, including a draft basis for the "principles governing future relations and a territorial settlement between Israel and each of her neighbors." In the course of considering a response to this draft document, the PCC embarked on the first steps of a process that was soon to produce the Lausanne Protocol. The next steps, undertaken in consultation with the Israeli delegation, were modeled deliberately on the methods that had been used by Ralph Bunche during the Rhodes talks. The principal secretary of the commission, Pablo de Azcárate, drafted a "Declaration of Principles" which was circulated unofficially to all delegations for comments. The PCC's aim was to use the "device of [a] preamble of general principle" on which both parties could agree to "create [a] favorable atmosphere and provide [a] point of departure for further discussions and for further agreement."[1]

During four days of informal discussions, a number of difficulties had to be overcome, including the "obstructive line" adopted by the Syrians (then in difficult armistice negotiations with Israel) against Arab agreement to discuss anything until satisfaction was obtained, in advance, on the return of the refugees.[2] Another obstacle was Israel's preference to use the map of the existing cease-fire lines, rather than the 1947 UN partition scheme being proposed by the PCC as a working document. Following much haggling and arm-twisting, the Israeli representative agreed to de Boisanger's proposal, "on the understanding that no communication [was] made to the press," and it being "clearly understood that this readiness in no way prejudice[d] the right of my delegation to express itself freely on matters at issue, on which it fully reserve[d] its position."[3] It was an open secret that the Israelis were being forced to sign a document which they considered unsatisfactory under duress of US pressure and in order to facilitate Israel's admission into the United Nations.[4]

During parallel PCC meetings with Israeli and Arab delegations on the morning of 12 May 1949, separate copies of a document known as the Lausanne Protocol were signed. At 10:30 a.m., Walter Eytan signed on behalf of Israel. At 11:30 a.m., Abd al-Mun'im Mustafa signed for Egypt, Fawzi al-Mulqi for Jordan, Fuad Ammoun for Lebanon and Adnan al-Atassi for Syria.[5] The short and "curious" document[6] was a masterpiece of diplomatic engineering. It said very little, but was significant in that it succeeded in marrying the refugee and boundaries issues. The first paragraph stated that, in the interest of achieving the objectives of the 11 December 1948 resolution regarding refugees as well as territorial questions, the PCC had submitted a "working document" — the November 1947 partition map adopted by the UNGA — "as a basis for discussions." The second paragraph announced the agreement of the delegations to cooperate with the commission "with the understanding that the exchanges of views... will bear upon the territorial adjustments necessary to implement the above-indicated objectives." In subsequent months and years the protocol would become a source of conflicting interpretation and recrimination. At the time, however, it served the very practical purpose of enabling the stalled Lausanne talks to proceed. It did so by responding to Arab insistence on making the refugee question the first priority while simultaneously acceding to Israeli wishes by unblocking the way to discussions on territorial issues.

Ten years after Lausanne, Eytan wrote bitterly that the protocol, "like so much else at Lausanne, was a sham."[7] Within weeks of the signature, Ambassador Eban informed Eytan that he believed it had been a mistake to sign the Lausanne Protocol; privately he was hoping to see the suspension of the PCC, and a "new start,... forgetting [the] protocol and other waste products."[8] While Eban's wish did not materialize, Israeli spokesmen immediately took to ignoring and undermining the protocol, characterizing the document as merely a "procedural device" and attributing no political significance to their country's signature (e.g., Eban's November letter to the PCC discussed below, pp. 112-13). Israel's main concern after 12 May seemed to be "how to appease the Americans in order to be able to undo the harm caused by the protocol."[9] Looking back in 1960, the Israel Office of Information announced that

> The protocols [*sic*] were neither "an agreement" nor "a covenant" between Israel and the Arab States, or between them, respectively, and the commission, to implement specific solutions to problems of boundaries, the internationalization of Jerusalem or any other matter in dispute. They were simply an agreement to discuss, to negotiate, each party reserving the right to state its own position.

In Israel's view, the one "outstanding aspect" of the Lausanne Protocol had been "the mutual recognition of each other's formal, legal, sovereign existence by the parties."[10]

In his memoirs, Ahmad Shuqayri referred to this historic document as being "Neither Fish nor Frog." He wrote mockingly of the commissioners' "total delight over this great triumph which [they] had achieved in the signing of the protocol." For his part, Shuqayri claimed it was "no stronger than the 1948 UN resolution" and that he didn't see "anything new in it." In informal conversation with the commissioners on 12 May, Shuqayri belittled the importance of obtaining Israel's signature on a document which committed the signatories to discussions based on the GA resolution of 11 December 1948 and on the 1947 partition map.[11]

As we shall see below, it was not long before Arab spokesmen began presenting their case to the PCC, the US and the world based on the protocol, accusing Israel of bad faith by failing to honor its signature which, they claimed, had amounted to official acceptance of the 1947 partition boundaries.[12] Consistent with this view, some Arab writers have used the Arabic translation *mithaq* when talking of the Lausanne Protocol, with the effect of elevating the importance of the document into a pact or covenant.[13] In later years, the Lausanne Protocol would serve as the starting point for occasional Arab feelers and trial balloons for a settlement with Israel.[14]

There can be no doubting the historical significance of the Arab delegates' signatures to the Lausanne Protocol. As Shuqayri himself later recalled, it was evidence of a change in Arab tactics, from a sterile "'No' complex" to a tactical "'positivism.'"... "Attached to that protocol," he wrote, "was the partition map to be a basis for discussion, and this was the partition which we had rejected in 1947 and 1948." Even though the Arab delegations remained "cautious, wary and on their guard so that there would be no recognition, surrender or yielding,... there could be no arguing or doubting that it was a step on the road to 'positivism.'"[15] Even Walter Eytan would not have disagreed; three days before the signing, the head of the Israeli delegation had recognized that it would be "a great thing for us if the Arabs, who had never been willing to touch November 29th with a barge pole, agreed to take this as a 'base de travail'." The Israeli official had, in fact, mistakenly predicted that the Arabs would never agree to sign.[16] But, while the Arabs proceeded to obtain much tactical mileage from their signatures to the Lausanne Protocol, many officials could still not bring themselves to state publicly and clearly that this meant that they now accepted the partition plan which they had rejected in 1947.[17]

Staking Out the Positions: The First Deadlock

Once the Lausanne Protocol was signed, interpretations differed as to what the document implied, and the operative question became: Where do we go from here? The existence and contents of the protocol remained secret for several weeks, which allowed each of the delegations to begin practical discussions quietly, while maintaining intact their opening public stances.[18] In the immediate wake of the signing of the protocol, the commission hoped to achieve progress by dividing its work into subcommittees, including a "general" committee (i.e., refugees and territorial issues) and one dealing with the internationalization of Jerusalem (under James Barco). Later a "technical" committee was formed to deal with practical matters relating to the return of refugees and the protection of their property.[19]

Soon enough a semblance of a bargaining situation emerged in which some offers and counter offers were transmitted from one party to the other using the PCC as postman or mail box. The Arab delegations' position papers predictably dealt almost exclusively with refugees, while those submitted by the Israeli delegation focused, also predictably, on territory. Equally quickly, however, it became obvious that the opening stances of the two sides were too far apart for successful reconciliation, and deadlock loomed. During their first post-protocol meeting with the PCC, the Israelis "startled" and "confused" the commissioners by taking a deliberately hard and legalistic stand on the withdrawal of all Arab forces from the territory of mandatory Palestine. During a meeting on 20 May, the Israeli delegation formally proposed to the PCC that the former Palestine-Lebanon and Palestine-Egypt frontiers should constitute Israel's future frontiers with Lebanon and Egypt, respectively.[20]

On 18 May, the Arab delegations addressed their own memorandum to the General Committee of the PCC, listing nine demands dealing with "urgent measures concerning the protection of the rights and property of the refugees."[21] Three days later, they reminded the commission that the "immediate execution of these measures was indispensable to the creation of an atmosphere favorable to the success of the conversations." In offering their general observations regarding the implementation of the protocol signed on 12 May, the Arab delegations went on to restate the position that the refugee problem was "of primary importance and that the solution recommended by the United Nations on 11 December 1948 must be put into effect in its entirety at the earliest possible moment." As a "first step toward this end," the Arab delegations pointed to the 1947 partition map — now initialed as a working document of the Lausanne Protocol — and urged that those refugees coming from the areas *outside* Israeli territory on that map "be enabled to return to their homes forthwith."[22]

After receiving the Arab memorandum of 18 May transmitted by the PCC, Walter Eytan forwarded it to his government for study, but not without taking the opportunity to write at length to the commission chairman to challenge "certain misconceptions" which seemed, to him, to underlie the Arab attitude. He warned against any "attempt to found a solution of the refugee problem on assumptions which [bore] little or no relation to fact," and proceeded to review the Israeli version of responsibility for the 1948 war and the changes that had come about during and since the fighting. "There can be no return to the *status quo ante*," he wrote on 25 May. "The clock cannot be turned back."

> If an Arab refugee counts upon living again in the house he abandoned, or plying his trade in the workshop he formerly rented, or tilling the fields in the vicinity of the village he once knew, he is living under an illusion which it seems to me essential to dispel. His house, his workshop, his village possibly no longer exist.

Eytan had taken the liberty of writing "with some frankness" because the Israeli delegation was "convinced that the success of the Lausanne talks depend[ed] upon a full understanding of the facts" which he outlined. The problem facing all the participants at Lausanne, as he defined it, was "how to solve the refugee problem on the basis of the existing situation." Any attempt to "recreate" the conditions of eighteen months or a year earlier would be "profitless and doomed to failure."

> Any wishful thinking on the part of the Arab delegations, any failure to realize that the situation is what it is, must act as a brake on the progress of our negotiations and ultimately lead to their collapse.

Eytan closed with the hope that those commissioners who negotiated with the Arab delegations would "take an opportunity of explaining... fully" to the Arabs "the situation as it exists at the present time and the consequences that flow from it."[23]

In a second letter of the same date, Eytan provided his delegation's observations on the contents of the second Arab memorandum as summarized by the PCC. These comments touched only incidentally on the specific demands in the Arab memorandum, but dealt rather with the fundamental gap which separated the approaches of the two sides. While Israel had always stressed the "organic link between the problems still outstanding," the Arab delegations had, "with equal consistency, refused to talk of an overall settlement and [had] concentrated their attention on one of the many problems that still await solution, wholly disregarding the others." He repeated Israel's willingness "to cooperate in the solution of the refugee problem... if this solution is seen organically as part of a final settlement between the Arab States and ourselves." The "ultimate objective" of the Lausanne talks, Eytan reiterated, "must be the establishment of permanent peacet"; within that context, Israel was prepared "to cooperate fully with the Arab delegations in finding a solution to the refugee problem." Hoping for the success of the deliberations, the head of the Israeli delegation suggested that the PCC undertake a "determined effort... to persuade the Arab Governments to face the problems at issue in a spirit of greater realism."

> To persist in making demands that bear no relation at all to realities cannot possibly advance the cause of the Arab States, and still less the cause of the refugees which they have at heart. Proposals such as those set out [in the Arab delegations' memorandum]... offer no sort of basis for negotiation.[24]

Although studiously avoiding any public criticism of the PCC's performance or personalities, the head of the Israeli delegation was clearly losing patience with the commission. In a telegraphic report of 21 May to Moshe Sharett, Walter Eytan wrote contemptuously of the PCC's lack of "guts" and "initiative" because of its hesitation over whether to inform the Arab delegations of Israel's territorial proposals. "All these weeks [at] Lausanne [had been] spent shadowboxing words and more words[,] with [the] commission unwilling or impotent [to] talk horse sense to [the] Arabs." Since Egypt and Lebanon had declared that they had "no territorial ambitions [in] Palestine," he failed to see why those countries should not find the proposal acceptable, and regretted that there was no evidence of the PCC "pressing" those delegations on the subject. Eytan also predicted that the Arab delegations' "insistence on talking refugees and nothing else at all, repeat, at all" would "sooner or later blow up [the] conference."[25] More than five years later, Eytan was still complaining that there was "not the slightest sign of the Arabs' being interested in the refugees except as a stick with which to beat Israel." In February 1955, the director general of the IMFA revealed his frustration and contempt for the persisting legacy of Ethridge's brief term on the PCC in a letter to a member of Israel's UN delegation. Should Israel be required, he asked rhetorically, to make "[a]nother unilateral gesture? Another vain attempt, *à la Ethridge*, to 'set the ball rolling,' to 'improve the atmosphere?' Personally," he concluded, he had "not the least little bit of faith in gestures or concessions, except as a means of appeasing the Western Powers that be."[26]

By this point in the proceedings Mark Ethridge was describing the situation at Lausanne as a "virtual stalemate," caused largely, in his view, by an Israeli delegation which had "stiffened" its demands.[27] He also found himself reacting to Eytan's approach by explaining that the PCC "could not be expected to embrace [the] views of either [party] for [the] purpose of persuading [the] other." With the blessing of the commission, he informed Eytan that some of his "assumptions and conclusions" were "at variance [with] my [i.e., Ethridge's] views and [there was] no useful purpose in discussion." Hoping for a breakthrough *via* another avenue, Ethridge suggested that Eytan formulate a statement destined for transmission to the Arab delegations. He believed that this would be an important development "for psychological reasons," since he expected that "Israeli views drafted with [the] Arabs rather than [the] UN in mind" would be "more temperate and persuasive."[28]

But no psychological breakthrough was to follow. For his part, Eytan became despondent about the lack of success of his "all-out effort" to persuade the PCC to "adopt a more workmanlike [and] realistic approach."[29] In response to PCC requests, Eytan summarized on 31 May Israel's stand on frontiers, refugees, and an international regime for Jerusalem, repeating that these issues were to be seen in the context of the Israeli delegation's "primary aim... to negotiate a final settlement of all questions outstanding between Israel and the Arab States, with a view to achieving permanent peace and continuing stability in the Middle East." With regard to refugees, Eytan referred to Israel's proposals for the inclusion of Gaza and its refugees into Israel (see below) and for family reunification. The return and rehabilitation of those refugees would be "subject to the conclusion of a final peace settlement between Israel and the Arab States." The Israeli delegation declared that it was "not within the capacity of Israel to resettle and rehabilitate all the refugees" (which it numbered at approximately 550,000), and that the Arab states should absorb all those not resettled in Israel.[30]

The continuing gap between the Israeli and Arab positions on the return of refugees (even if the latter was seen by the Israelis and others as more tactical than principled) was not the only area of dispute at Lausanne. Direct contacts in Paris between members of the Israeli and Lebanese delegations soon confirmed the existence of an equally unbridgeable gap between the Arab states and Israel on territorial issues.[31] From the Arabs' point of view, their signing of the Lausanne Protocol and the positions outlined in their memoranda of 18 and 21 May constituted serious concessions which had not been reciprocated by the Israelis. "On the contrary," the Jordanian delegate complained to Mark Ethridge, "the Jews ha[d] given nothing and [were] demanding more. No Arab politician could dare to make any further concessions." Jordan's Fawzi al-Mulqi also invoked negative public opinion in the wake of the humiliation of the armistice agreements as a factor limiting the Arab delegates' room for maneuver at Lausanne. His own country's attitude had "hardened considerably" in the wake of Israel's "excessive gunpoint demands" regarding the handing over of territory in the Tulkarm triangle, in accordance with the armistice signed on 3 April, and lingering disputes in the Jerusalem area. In hopes of avoiding the breakup of the conference, Mulqi announced that he would raise the possibility with his Arab colleagues of asking the commission to submit its own proposals to the parties.[32]

CHAPTER 6

Attempts to Break the Deadlock: Israel's Gaza Offer

Presidential Rebuke to Israel

The PCC remained reluctant to provide Arabs and Israelis with its own proposals for a solution. But several other attempts were made at this time in an effort to break the lingering post-protocol deadlock. American pressure reached its highest point in attempts to persuade Israel to agree to declare its readiness to repatriate a significant number of refugees and to procure Arab agreement to large-scale resettlement of those who would not be returned to Israel-held territory. On 29 May, Ambassador J. G. McDonald delivered a stern, accusatory message from President Truman to Prime Minister Ben-Gurion, underlining the divergences between the American/United Nations policy and that of Israel regarding a territorial settlement and the refugee question. "The Government of the United States," Truman began, was "seriously disturbed by the attitude of Israel...," and he expressed his "deep concern" that American representations over the preceding months had "made so little impression upon the Government of Israel." The note warned, "in candor," that "the rigid attitude of the Government of Israel" was liable to cause a "rupture" of the Lausanne talks, and concluded ominously:

> If the Government of Israel continues to reject the basic principles set forth by the resolution of the General Assembly of Dec. 11, 1948 and the friendly advice offered by the US Government for the sole purpose of facilitating a genuine peace in Palestine, the US Government will regretfully be forced to the conclusion that a

revision of its attitude toward Israel has become unavoidable.[1]

The presidential note was the second direct US-Israel confrontation regarding the Lausanne peace process (after the Acheson-Shertok meeting in New York) and caused the most severe strain in relations between the two countries since the founding of the state. Israeli representatives in Tel Aviv, Washington and New York devoted much of the following weeks to "damage control" and to reestablishing their credibility and good faith in American eyes. These efforts must have had their impact, as evidenced in the remark of the American ambassador in Israel that "[t]he next few months marked a steady retreat from the intransigence of the United States May note," as well as a disinclination to "lay down the law to Tel Aviv" or to suggest solutions to either side.[2] The Jewish state's ability to withstand American and British criticism and pressure without significant loss of political and economic support left Arab observers scandalized, concluding that diplomatic gestures on the part of the powers were "empty of any real substance."[3]

Israel's Offer to Incorporate the Gaza Strip

Towards the end of May, Israeli representatives at Lausanne undertook several initiatives aimed at getting the talks moving again. On 27 May Dr. Eytan suggested that the PCC "in effect lift [the] refugee question out of [the] context of [the] Lausanne meetings" by proposing its own "imaginative broad plan" for refugee resettlement. This proposal — an Israeli version of the McGhee plans then under consideration in Washington — was, to Ethridge's mind, an unacceptable attempt to relieve the principal parties of their primary responsibility for a solution while asking the international community to "pick up the check." He lectured Dr. Eytan on the likely conditions which an international refugee scheme would impose upon Israelis and Arabs, reminding him of his view that the "key to peace" was, as it had been since January, in Israel's hands.[4]

A more serious Israeli proposal to incorporate "the Gaza area and its present Arab population" into Israel was taken up in earnest by Eytan on 29 May[5] — the very day the presidential rebuke was being handed to Ben-Gurion. The suggestion had been advanced in Lausanne ten days earlier and, for some reason, seems to have gone unnoticed by both the president and State Department.[6] The origins of this proposal go back most probably to Israeli political circles in March-April 1949.[7] During his wide-ranging conversation with Mark Ethridge in Tiberias on 18 April, David Ben-Gurion had suggested the possibility that the "present Gaza Strip might become autonomous like Luxembourg. If Egypt did not want Gaza because of [the] refugees therein," Ethridge reported Ben-Gurion as saying, "Israel would accept and permit those refugees to return to their homes."[8] Israeli officials subsequently weighed the advantages and drawbacks of annexing Gaza — while at times attempting to attribute the authorship of the idea to Mark Ethridge.[9]

The American representative on the PCC was indeed a strong supporter of the idea, as he had admitted to Walter Eytan during their first informal meeting at Lausanne.[10] Responding to Eytan's request for guidance, the matter was brought before the Israeli cabinet on 3 May, when a majority voted (with Sharett among the dissenters) that "should the annexation to the state of the Gaza Strip with all its inhabitants be proposed, our answer will be positive."[11]

The Israeli delegation at Lausanne then waited for an opportunity to respond to a Gaza proposition emanating from Ethridge or elsewhere, preferring to avoid the appearance of too direct an Israeli initiative. When, after several weeks, this did not happen, the Israeli delegation chose to assume responsibility for advancing the Gaza offer. The territorial proposals which Israel made to the PCC on 20 May clearly implied taking over the Gaza Strip, thereby making, as Eytan argued, a "notable contribution towards [a] solution [of the] refugee problem." Eytan was appalled that the PCC was hesitant about transmitting the proposals to the Egyptians. On 27 May, Eytan met with the PCC and, in the course of defending his country's stand on repatriation against American criticism, reminded the commissioners of Israel's standing offer to incorporate Gaza.[12]

Two days later, Eytan wrote to PCC Chairman de Boisanger to elaborate on Israel's Gaza proposal, touting its advantages as a practical way of ending the misery of "the people now herded in the Gaza Strip" and giving them "a hope of rebuilding their lives."[13] On 30 May, the Arab delegations informed the PCC that they considered Israel's territorial proposals, including the Gaza offer, to be a "flagrant violation of the terms of the Protocol of 12 May."[14] The following day, the comprehensive summary of Israel's stand on frontiers and refugees drawn up for the PCC was still built around the proposal to incorporate the Gaza area into Israel, which would become responsible for the rehabilitation and resettlement of "all the refugees now in that area."[15]

One Israeli historian has labeled the Gaza plan "a mirage" — but one which "riveted the attention of policy-makers in Washington," holding out "the promise of a miraculous deliverance" from the stalemate at Lausanne.[16] Indeed, during the months of June and July, unexpected support for Israel's Gaza proposal came from the US State Department, where officials began to look on it as a possible key to unblocking the stalled negotiations. The proposal managed to sustain the serious interest of Dean Acheson and the State Department during this period thanks to a combination of wishful thinking and confusing signals as to whether the Egyptians would be willing to contemplate such a territory-cum-refugee arrangement. Not only was State Department optimism maintained in the face of growing indications of Egyptian rejection, but a decision was made to risk American political capital by offering American good offices to the Egyptians and Israelis for the purpose of discussing the Gaza proposal.

On 4 June, the State Department informed the US delegation at Lausanne that the American government would approve the incorporation of Gaza into Israel "as part [of a] final territorial settlement provided this c[ou]ld be achieved by negot[iation] with and full consent [of the] Egyptian Gov[ernmen]t and provided territorial compensation [was] made to Egypt according [to the] Pres[ident]'s formula [i.e., the "Jessup principle"] if Egypt desires such compensation." The State Department also listed several measures designed to protect the rights of the refugees and residents of Gaza. Several days later, the US ambassador in Tel Aviv was instructed to inform the Israeli government that the US saw "no reason why [the] area might not be incorporated" into Israel, with the same provisos regarding negotiation and the possible exchange of territory.[17]

As for Egyptian reactions, American sources in Cairo were indicating in early June that "Egypt might well be willing [to] cede Gaza," along with its "refugee burden," in the course of future bargaining.[18] Mark Ethridge's return to Washington gave added momentum to the State Department's pursuit of the Gaza proposal as a good basis for a territorial, not just a refugee, settlement — "providing that it [was] accompanied by a *quid pro quo*: some part of the Negev."[19] For their part, the Israelis sought to maintain the impression, for the Americans and for the PCC, that the Egyptians were not particularly interested in retaining Gaza. Eytan tried to persuade Ethridge that the Egyptians would rather turn the strip over to Israel than to Jordan's Abdallah.[20]

But contradictory signals about Egyptian intentions regarding the Gaza Strip abounded. The Jordanian delegate told the PCC representative that he felt the Egyptians would prefer to "give it to nobody."[21] An internal Israeli report from Eliahu Sasson quoted the head of the Egyptian delegation at Lausanne as stating categorically that:

> Not only would Egypt not cede the Gaza area, but she would also insist on receiving the Negev south of a line between Majdal and the Dead Sea.... Egypt strongly rejects Ethridge's plan *[sic]* for Gaza and its refugees.[22]

In subsequent meetings at Lausanne, Sasson received confirmation of both Egypt's and Jordan's categorical rejection of the idea.[23] Independent British sources also reported evidence that the Egyptians would be reluctant to abandon the Gaza Strip, with one source underlining Egypt's psychological need to keep the territory as the "sole tangible trophy of [the] Palestine campaign."[24]

State Department support for Ethridge's line of thinking persisted even in the face of increasingly clear official Egyptian signals that the plan was a nonstarter. For example, on 10 June, the Egyptian ambassador in Washington called on Acting Secretary Webb to press for the lifting of the Middle East arms embargo. When the acting secretary raised Israel's Gaza proposal, the ambassador stated that the Egyptian government regarded it as "cheap barter." He suggested that the first step should be for Israel to allow those refugees who wished to return to do so; following this, Egypt would be prepared to negotiate minor frontier adjustments in an effort to achieve strategically defensible borders for both countries. In cabling the contents of the conversation to the US Embassy in Cairo, Webb instructed the American *chargé d'affaires* to sound out Egyptian government views for greater certainty.[25]

The reply from Cairo confirmed the negative attitude expressed by the Egyptian ambassador. Foreign Minister Khashaba was reported as making it clear that Egypt would "not be willing [to] cede [the] Gaza strip to Israel even if Israel sh[ou]ld agree [to] relieve Egypt of [the] refugee burden [in] that area."[26] Meanwhile, in Lausanne, the Arab delegations once again rejected the Gaza proposal, this time stressing to the PCC that they considered it as contrary to UNGA resolution 194 of 11 December 1948.[27]

American Good Offices Offered to Israel and Egypt

Despite such negative reactions, Abba Eban was able to report in mid-June that the Gaza proposal still attracted State Department officials, and recommended that it should therefore be kept to the fore. Ambiguous signals from Abd al-Mun'im Mustafa to Mark Ethridge just prior to the latter's departure from Lausanne added to the confusion, and served to keep the Gaza proposal alive during the coming month. Ethridge's advice to Dean Rusk in favor of exploiting the potential of Israel's Gaza offer seems to have helped to convince the State Department to continue pursuing that avenue.[28]

On 24 June, an *aide-mémoire* handed to the Israeli *chargé d'affaires* in Washington repeated the US government's hopeful position that it saw "no reason why the [Gaza] proposal might not become the basis for discussions between the Government of Israel and other interested Governments." In his accompanying remarks to Uriel Heyd, Dean Rusk went further, indicating that "the Gaza strip proposal was perhaps the key which would unlock the whole problem." For this reason, the State Department was "most anxious that the Egyptians and Israelis get together and see what could be worked out." The Israelis, Rusk added, might wish to utilize the contacts they already had with the Egyptians. "(O)n the other hand[,] if these were not satisfactory we were willing to help in arranging an exchange of views."[29]

Thus began the brief episode of America's offer of its good offices (sometimes erroneously referred to as its offer of "mediation") to Israel and to Egypt to discuss the Gaza proposal. Believing that British advice to the Egyptians carried great weight, Acheson immediately appealed to the Foreign Office for backing of the plan as "the only means [for] breaking [the] Israeli-Arab *impasse re* refugees" in the context of "common US-UK objectives." He regarded Egyptian interest in "frontier rectifications" in the Negev as the key bargaining chip, and proposed to "take [a] strong line with [the] Egyptians, based on [the] overriding consideration of getting constructive action *re* refugees." The US secretary of state "urgently request[ed the] firmest UK support for these representations" for the Gaza plan, and also for moderating Egypt's "unrealistic attitude" regarding specific frontier demands.[30]

The British reaction was disappointingly lukewarm. One official took the cynical view that the Gaza plan was a "subtle" one that "would give the Israelis something for nothing in the way of territory and would not prevent them from driving the Arabs out of the area after they had occupied it."[31] The Foreign Office replied to Washington that it "did not wish to give Egypt advice one way or [the] other" regarding territorial adjustments, and was "inclined to think it would be better for Egypt to keep [the] Gaza strip and its refugees and for Israel to take another 150,000 refugees from elsewhere."[32]

Reacting to the Foreign Office rebuff, Acheson instructed the American ambassador in London to inform Foreign Secretary Ernest Bevin that the US government was "disturbed by" the British attitude to the Gaza proposal. In contrast to the British view, the Americans believed that any "strategic advantages" of Egypt's retaining Gaza would "appear to be outweighed by [the] administrative burden and enormous financial requirements" of maintaining the refugee population. Elaborating on the proposed *quid pro quo*, Acheson affirmed that the US was "prepared to support politically feasible modifications [of the] Egyptian frontier in return for cession [of the] Gaza strip with all [its] present occupants to Israel." This approach to an overall settlement, the US believed, "constitute[d a] firmer basis for [the] strategic security of all states concerned" than could be achieved through Egypt's exploitation of "minor military advantages" by keeping the strip. The US was "firmly convinced" that the Gaza proposal should become a "basis for discussion between Egypt and Israel," as this would "probably pave [the] way for [an] Israeli-Egyptian final settlement and thereby constitute [a] decisive step towards [an] overall Palestine settlement." The secretary of state closed by reiterating the United States' "urgent request for firm UK support" of its efforts to gain Egypt's cooperation.[33]

Acheson would find even less satisfaction from his representations to the Egyptians, who were now subjected to increasing American pressure to discuss the Gaza proposal. His instructions to his *chargé* in Cairo were to express firmly to the Egyptian foreign minister the US government's "profound disappointment" in the "negative attitude" which Egypt had been showing regarding the refugee problem. The Arab states, Acheson warned, should give "most serious attention to [the] consequences during recent years of their steadfast refusal [to] accept [the] realities [of the] situation *re* Pal[estine]." Brandishing the sole American "stick" for persuading the Egyptians, the secretary of state pointed ominously to the uncertain future of refugee relief funding (most of it coming from US charitable organizations), and noted that Egypt had thus far failed to provide information regarding its plans for the permanent disposition of the refugees in Gaza. By contrast, the Israelis had undertaken to "assume full responsibility" for the refugees and residents if that area were incorporated into Israel as part of a settlement. As such, Acheson concluded, the Israeli proposal should

> be given most serious and constructive consideration by [the] Egyptian Gov[ernmen]t. [The p]roposal sh[ou]ld serve as [a] basis [for] urgent discussion between [the] states concerned, through direct or indirect negot[iation]s.

The US government was prepared to "lend all possible assistance [to] facilitate such negot[iation]s."[34]

During his meeting with Foreign Minister Khashaba on 27 June, *Chargé* Patterson's mention of Egypt's "negative attitude" elicited a sharp retort. How, asked Khashaba, could "Egypt's steady insistence on [the] positive implementation of numerous UN resolutions" be called "negative"? The minister, who frequently interrupted Patterson "in a rather agitated fashion," became particularly annoyed at the US view of the refugee problem being "a joint responsibility" of the Arab states and Israel. The Israeli proposal for Gaza, in Khashaba's view, "amounted to their insistence on being paid for fulfilling a prior obligation imposed upon them by [the] UN," and he feared that Gaza's refugee population would be "turned off in all probability into the desert of the Negev." In conclusion, however, the minister stated that Egypt "would not refuse to give serious consideration to any plan designed as [a] humanitarian measure and susceptible of bringing stability to an area or situation." He requested a written brief of the US position.[35]

On 28 June, Secretary Acheson authorized the transmission of an *aide-mémoire* to the Egyptian government along the lines of his earlier instructions to Patterson, with the following additional considerations:

a. The US government "note[d] with appreciation" the foreign minister's assurances that Egypt was prepared to give "serious consideration" to the plan, and was "firmly convinced" that the Gaza proposal formed the basis of an "important contribution to [a] final settlement" of the Palestine problem as well as a "constructive approach to [a] solution [of the] grave humanitarian problem of [the] refugees."

b. In response to the foreign minister's expressed concerns for the welfare of the refugees under future Israeli rule, the US was prepared to seek information regarding Israeli plans for their resettlement and to advocate the establishment of "appropriate international supervision."

c. The US government "recall [ed] with deep appreciation" Egypt's "constructive action" as the first state to conclude an armistice agreement with Israel, and was "deeply hopeful" that Egypt was "now prepared [to] give [a] similar stimulus to [a] final settlement [of the] outstanding issues by entering into early discussions with Israel *re* Gaza proposal."

The US *aide-mémoire* reiterated that, "if so requested," the United States stood "ready to facilitate such discussions by all [the] means at its disposal."[36] It would be only after the Lausanne recess that the Egyptian government would reply definitively to the American offer of good offices for Egyptian-Israeli discussion of the Gaza proposal.

CHAPTER 7

June Stalemate and Adjournment

While soundings continued in Washington, London and Cairo regarding the feasibility of the Gaza proposal, the delegations in Lausanne continued their maneuvering and shadowboxing without progress. The Lebanese foreign minister was reported to be "despondent" over the course of the Lausanne talks, and accused the Israelis of acting in bad faith. The feeling in Damascus, as reported by UN officials, was that Lausanne would fail and that fighting might soon be resumed.[1] After a week in Tel Aviv, Walter Eytan returned to find "the general sense of failure... beginning to get on people's nerves."[2] The head of the Israeli delegation found Ethridge particularly irritated upon realizing that Israel "had conceded nothing under pressure of the President's note." Eytan met with the commission on 9 June, and, in Ethridge's words,

> lectured [the] PCC at length on [the] manner in which talks should be conducted and made [a] general restatement of [the] Israeli position.... Eytan's remarks indicated [that] Israel had not modified its position in any way, shape or form.

But, just as convinced as Ethridge was about Israel's alleged unreasonableness, Eytan was equally certain that it was the Arabs' unrealistic demands for the return of refugees and their "refusal... to negotiate peace" which were the "main cause" of the Lausanne deadlock. Recapitulating Israel's various proposals and suggestions, he expressed his disappointment in the absence of any Arab responses. Israel would be prepared to make further suggestions (such as the creation of a free port at Haifa) if that were deemed useful. Israel's efforts at Lausanne had been, he claimed, "fundamentally different" from Arab efforts which had consisted "entirely of demands." Eytan concluded by offering to state the Israeli case directly to Arab delegates.[3]

On his last day in Lausanne, Mark Ethridge reported no progress in reconciling Arab and Israeli positions and no possibility in the immediate future of obtaining commitments from the parties regarding repatriation and resettlement. These commitments were considered necessary by American officials to pave the way for the work of the proposed Economic Survey Group. Ethridge left Lausanne "in a mood of great bitterness," mostly against the Israelis, although, Eytan conceded, "fair-minded enough to admit that the Arabs' attitude was unrealistic."[4]

At a subsequent meeting with the PCC on 11 June, Eytan elaborated on some of his earlier comments and suggestions for breaking the *impasse* at Lausanne. One of his proposals was for a PCC official to pay a flying visit to Arab capitals in order to obtain enlarged mandates for the Lausanne delegations to discuss matters beyond the narrowly-defined refugee issue. Eytan also quoted from the six-month-old UNGA resolution 194 to suggest that the PCC had not done enough to help establish "direct contact between the parties themselves... at the earliest possible date." He also proposed the reorganization of work from the "general" subcommittee of the PCC (which included territorial matters and refugees) into three more carefully defined subcommittees. Finally, Eytan suggested greater reliance on the armistice agreements as bases for the discussions at Lausanne. Although he claimed before the commissioners that this request did not contradict the Lausanne Protocol, Eytan confessed to Sharett that his "main purpose" behind this suggestion was precisely "to begin to undermine the protocol of 12 May, which we had signed only under... duress." The members of the commission offered their unfavorable reactions to the four Israeli suggestions, leaving Eytan disappointed by this "cavalier rejection" of proposals "which had obviously been produced after a good deal of thought."[5]

By this point, Eytan was growing weary of the PCC's "*idée fixe*" with regard to the Israeli position, which he characterized as follows:

> If only you [Israelis] would accept the principle of repatriation, everything would be fine and dandy, and we'd get along like a house on fire. But as long as you maintain your obstinate, stubborn, rigid (choose your epithet) refusal, we are in no position to get the Arabs talking on other things, and there's no prospect of peace. You — Israel — are the ones who are preventing peace, and it's no good your saying you want peace. We don't believe you, because if you really want peace, you know how to get it. All you have to do is to declare your acceptance of the repatriation principle.[6]

After Ethridge left for Washington with suggestions for adjourning the Lausanne talks, Eytan met informally with the commissioners on 13 June. The Israeli delegate disagreed with the suggestion by the acting head of the American delegation, Raymond Hare, that the next move was Israel's. Dr. Eytan renewed his country's complaint at the continuing absence of direct meetings with Arab delegations and pointed out that Israel's Gaza proposal was still awaiting comment from the Arab side. Eytan aroused a glimmer of optimism among the commissioners when he wondered out loud about the likely Arab reaction if Israel — hypothetically — were to accept the principle of repatriation. Throwing the ball back into the Israeli court, Yalçin suggested that Israel's "acceptance in principle contingent on numerous provisos would provide [the] Arabs with [a] point of departure" for subsequent "constructive" discussions. Hare stressed the need for a "preliminary agreement of both sides" which would allow international agencies to prepare the practical basis for a resolution of the refugee question.[7]

The next day, Israeli delegates attending a formal meeting of the general committee of the PCC "dispelled any hope which Eytan's statements... might have contained." In replying to three of the specific demands in the Arab delegations' memoranda of 18 and 21 May, Sasson and Hirsch stuck close to the official Israeli line that the return of refugees could not be considered separately from an overall peace settlement. After "long involved discussion" it also became clear that the Arab and Israeli delegations were basing themselves on incompatible interpretations of the meaning of the protocol signed on 12 May.[8] During the following week, Eytan submitted three formal letters to the PCC, (a) clarifying the Israeli stand on a plebiscite to determine the fate of the Arab areas of Palestine, (b) requesting the commission to clarify whether the negotiating mandates for the Arab delegations were broad enough to allow discussion of more than the refugee issue, and (c) elaborating on his proposals to reorganize the committee structure of the commission.[9] Finally, on 27 June, after frequent postponements on the grounds that the matter was receiving "careful and sympathetic attention" in Tel Aviv, Eytan provided the PCC with Israel's official — but hardly sympathetic — reply to the Arab delegations' nine-point memorandum of 18 May.[10]

As far as the Arabs were concerned, "the Israeli delegation was procrastinating and hesitating, waiting for instructions, issuing statements and completing clarifications... while we were in a hurry, on pins and needles."[11] The PCC's meeting with the Arab delegations on 17 June was held under the shadow of Moshe Sharett's widely-publicized Knesset speech of 15 June,[12] which produced, according to American representative Hare, a "bitter 'what[']s the use' mood" among the Arab delegates. During the meeting, the Arab delegations announced that, until progress was made regarding their memoranda of 18 and 21 May, no other questions could be discussed. Israel was portrayed as not only evasive on the return of refugees, but also as acting in bad faith *vis-à-vis* UN resolutions and displaying expansionist tendencies. The Arabs considered themselves as having taken "progressive steps" by signing the 12 May protocol "unlike [the] Jews... without reservation."[13] At a further meeting on 25 June, the Arab delegations indicated their willingness to discuss territorial matters "if [the] Israeli delegation returned to [the] protocol of 12 May by basing its proposals upon it and if [the] PCC undertook to pass judgment on Israeli and presumably Arab proposals in connection therewith."[14]

On 18 June, the State Department advised Hare that, after the fullest consultation with Ethridge, it was recommending the PCC adjourn for two or three weeks "during which delegations w[ou]ld have [a] fresh opportunity [to] consult their gov[ernmen]ts with [a] view to advancing constructive proposals upon reconvening [in] Lausanne." It was hoped that, in the interim, both sides would be "free to have any negotiations, direct or otherwise," and to submit new proposals to the PCC.[15]

The move came as no surprise. Speculation had already been brewing about the possible suspension of the talks, with both sides admitting their futility but no one wishing to be "placed in [a] position of causing [the] break."[16] The departing American chief representative on the PCC had his own clear-cut and consistent views on this subject. Reporting from Paris *en route* to Washington, Mark Ethridge's assessment of the Lausanne stalemate laid "primary responsibility" on Israel, and blamed it for having consistently avoided the requested important concessions on refugees. Ethridge made no secret of his view that Israel's attitude toward the refugees had been both "morally reprehensible and politically short-sighted.... Her position as conqueror demanding more [did] not make for peace." There had "never been a time in the life of the commission," he concluded, "when a generous and far-sighted attitude on the part of the Jews would not have unlocked [the door to] peace."[17]

On 13 June, the commission's *Third Progress Report* to the UN summarized the irreconcilable positions of the parties on refugees, territory, and Jerusalem more even-handedly and delicately. Its conclusions contained an admission, in typically understated phrases, that the PCC now found itself having to "arrest" the "tendency" towards failure of the talks.[18]

CHAPTER 8

Activity during the Recess

Fine-tuning of the American, Israeli and Arab Positions

Just prior to the decision to recess the Lausanne talks, some American officials wondered whether, beyond the continuing need for a "firm line" and pressure on the Israelis, the time had come for "making strong specific suggestions [to] both sides, particularly *re* boundaries and refugees."[1] The case for greater American involvement of this sort was reinforced by Raymond Hare, who doubted whether the proposed short break and a return to Lausanne would, by themselves, lead to anything more than negotiations "renewed... on essentially [the] same basis as [the] present *impasse.*" The "basic fact, of course," he wrote, was that "neither side [was] actually ready for peace at this time."[2]

During the recess of the Lausanne talks (1-18 July), the State Department considered possible measures which might lead to a breakthrough of the stalemate into which the conference had sunk. On 13 July, Assistant Secretary George McGhee submitted a proposal for strengthening US support for the PCC efforts at Lausanne. Citing, in particular, the danger to regional stability of a prolongation and deterioration of the refugee problem, McGhee argued that it was "essential in the national interest that the United States Government take the initiative in an effort to overcome the present *impasse* in the negotiations for the settlement of the Palestine question." His recommendations fell short of advocating any specific solutions to the territorial and other issues, but dealt mainly with how the US

might assist the PCC in persuading the main protagonists to be more forthcoming. McGhee also proposed the speedy creation and despatch of an Economic Survey Mission to make an authoritative study of the numbers, distribution and conditions of the refugees.[3] In the spirit of McGhee's recommendations, instructions were sent to US missions in France, Turkey and all Middle Eastern capitals, affirming American determination to strengthen the PCC and appealing to all parties to return to Lausanne "with a new and constructive approach" and with "full authority... to enter into discussion and negotiation of all issues which fall within [the] purview of [the] PCC."[4]
The remainder of American diplomatic activity during the recess was focused on three specific projects:

a. For a while, the US continued to press for direct Egyptian-Israeli talks on the Israeli offer to incorporate Gaza, in the hope that such discussions would provide the key to a breakthrough on other issues. (below, pp. 78-86).
b. At the same time, the State Department displayed cautious interest in British suggestions for joint backing of a scheme for a settlement to be proposed through the PCC (below, pp. 86-88).
c. The appointment of Paul A. Porter, a Washington lawyer reported to have close ties with the president, as chief US representative on the PCC was meant to appear as evidence of American determination to strengthen the commission's chances of success.[5]

During the recess of the Lausanne talks, the Israeli Cabinet and Foreign Ministry both devoted much attention to reformulating Israeli strategy with a view to improving the conference's chances of success and avoiding a renewal of the Palestine debate at the UNGA in the fall. On 5 July, the cabinet defined the maximum numbers of refugees it would allow in both cases of incorporating, and of not incorporating, Gaza — thereby setting the stage for the offer to repatriate 100,000 (see below, pp. 92-95).[6] On 7 July, the government of Israel officially announced administrative details of its family reunification scheme, following the policy statement made earlier by the foreign minister in the Knesset. In conveying this information to the PCC at Lausanne,

Gershon Hirsch pointed out that this represented "a substantial relaxation of the principle that any return of Arab refugees to Israel must take place within the framework of a general settlement which assures peace and security to the State of Israel."[7] The terms of the offer appeared, to the State Department, scaled-down somewhat from the original, and Acheson feared that the Israelis might have no intention of moving any closer than this to committing themselves to large-scale repatriation. Still, the United States "welcome[d] this first tangible step toward commencement [of] the immediate repatriation long requested by [the] US G[overnment]," and expressed the hope that Israel would make "every effort [to] enlarge [the] scope [of] this process."[8]

Among the Arab states, Syria, in particular, seemed to be seeking American goodwill at this time, having accepted American advice on a compromise formula which had finally brought the Syrian-Israeli armistice negotiations to an end on 20 July. Owing to internal instability in Syria and special difficulties relating to the cease-fire lines,the Syrian-Israeli talks had been especially tortuous and protracted. Prime Minister Muhsin Barazi now reacted favorably to Acheson's exhortations for a more constructive attitude at Lausanne and contemplated making changes to the instructions for, and membership in, his country's delegation. The prime minister went further, suggesting that "he would use his influence with other Arab states to get them to adopt [a] more positive attitude." The American legation in Damascus dared to hope that Syria might now offer the "best Arab leadership in reaching [an] overall peace settlement."[9] The State Department seemed favorably impressed with Barazi's stand on Lausanne, which formed part of the brief US-Syrian "honeymoon" period under US protégé Husni Za'im.[10] The Jordanian foreign minister likewise informed the US *chargé d'affaires* in Amman that he had instructed his Lausanne delegation to discuss all outstanding issues without regard to previous Arab priorities.[11]

Pursuing the Gaza Proposal

The fact that the US had offered its good offices in the attempt to enlist Egyptian cooperation in the Gaza scheme was seen by Israelis as a mixed blessing. In New York, Abba Eban was enthusiastic, but Foreign Minister Sharett sought further advice from Lausanne on how to resolve the dilemma created by (a) the positive opportunity for successful and separate talks with the most important Arab state, and (b) the negative pressure of the known US position on the return of Israeli-held territory in the southern Negev.[12] In his reply to Sharett's query, Eytan confessed that he too found this an unresolvable dilemma. He saw the obvious dangers of the American offer to mediate, yet he recognized strong reasons for a positive Israeli response, which he expected would be an almost certain guarantee of successful mediation, which would be followed by the other Arab states "fall[ing] into line" and which would result in keeping the Palestine question off the agenda of the UN General Assembly in the fall. Although, according to first reports from Washington, the Israelis were free to decide whether or not they wished to take advantage of American good offices on this issue, Eytan felt that it was "practically impossible" for the Israelis to refuse the US offer without damaging their own general credibility, as well as their stock of goodwill in the US.[13]

In weighing the pros and cons of accepting US good offices — which, for all practical purposes, meant involving the Americans in a mediation role — Eytan was under no illusions about the price which Israel would have to pay. As *Chargé d'affaires* Heyd had first reported it to Sharett,[14] the State Department's Dean Rusk had clearly stated that territorial compensation for Egypt, and perhaps also "another Arab state," would be required. Speculating on the US-Egyptian dimension of the proposed mediation, Eytan could not imagine how Israel could "make peace with the Egyptians under USA negotiation [*sic?*] without giving up the Elath [Eilat] coast [at least]." If Israel "had been willing to give this up," he added, "we could have finished with all the Arabs here at Lausanne long ago."

> The Americans have put us on the spot all right [Eytan concluded]. If we say no, then we are the ones that don't want peace. If we say yes, we lose Elath. I don't believe the Americans would have proposed mediation, nor could they get the Egyptians to accept it, if it were not clear from the start that we should be forced to make this territorial concession.[15]

Several days later, Eliahu Sasson confirmed that the Arab delegations at Lausanne were under the impression that the Americans would back their claims to territorial concessions in the southern Negev.[16]

Despite Israeli misgivings and uncertainties, Foreign Minister Sharett sent a positive response to the State Department's offer of assistance in bringing about conversations with the Egyptians on the Gaza proposal.[17] In flushing out Israel's position on possible talks with Egypt, Abba Eban stressed the need to avoid showing "any sign [of] eagerness for Gaza." Israel should present its offer to take over Gaza and its refugee burden as a contribution to peace, but "if Egypt insists [on] retention, we would sign peace on [the] present armistice line[,] in which case Egypt accepts all refugees." If, on the other hand, Gaza were ceded to Israel, Eban proposed that "we would look with sympathy [on a] territorial adjustment [of a] similar area [on the] Sinai-Palestine border" — but "not including Eilat," which was "in no circumstances surrenderable."[18]

Israeli optimism about the Americans' ability to bring the Egyptians to the table was, as we shall see, ill-founded. And, as rational or consistent as the Israeli bargaining position on the Gaza offer was, it was inherently weakened by at least two factors. One was the negative perception, already current among Israel's Arab and other critics, that the offer was little more than an ominous, expansionist land-grab. Israeli arguments for incorporation of the Gaza Strip as an enhancement of Israel's security position, although directed to the State Department,[19] did nothing to offset the negative Arab perception of the Israeli offer. Despite the fact that it was now the *Americans*, rather than the Israelis, who were actively pushing the proposal, the Arab view of Israel's ulterior motives was not easily reversed. A senior Egyptian foreign ministry official not only regarded the Gaza scheme "as an indication of Israeli predatory intent," but also stated that "as long as Israelis felt they could obtain American support, they would never accept any proposition from any quarter."[20] Patterson reported from Cairo that American backing for the plan had contributed to "a growing suspicion of [the] inability or unwillingness of [the] USG to view [the] Palestine controversy impartially."[21]

The second element undermining the chances of success was the Israeli-American disagreement, glossed over at first, regarding the need for territorial compensation to Egypt, preferably in the Aqaba area, to create a land bridge between Egypt and Jordan. Eventually Israel had to make known its utter opposition to such territorial compensation.[22] The issue was further complicated by suspicions, held by many Israelis as well as members of the PCC, that a land corridor between Egypt and Jordan was more of a *British* strategic interest than a legitimate Arab demand or need.[23] These factors would again come into play during the 1950 Israeli-Jordanian negotiations for a peace treaty that would have provided Abdallah with a Negev corridor, as well as during the 1955-56 Anglo-American attempts at promoting an Egyptian-Israeli peace settlement.

Throughout the month of July, the State Department tried to persuade the Egyptians to agree to discuss the Gaza proposal, and somehow managed to maintain a shaky optimism despite increasingly negative signals from Cairo and elsewhere. On 1 July, Acheson cabled to Cairo, in the hopes that the *aide-mémoire* of 28 June (above, pp. 68-69) had received a positive reply, thereby enabling Egyptian representatives to proceed to meet with Israeli representatives at Lake Success. On the same day, the secretary also cabled London to request support from the British embassy in Egypt, and on 8 July the State Department informed the French and Turkish members of the PCC in Lausanne. Even though they were well aware of the gap separating the two sides, State Department officials were reported still "hopeful" of possible success at using the Gaza proposal to "break [... the] entire ice."[24]

But, on 7 July, the first of several decidedly negative reports arrived from Cairo. In a conversation with American *Chargé* Patterson, the undersecretary at the Egyptian Foreign Ministry "reacted vigorously" to the former's suggestion that Israel's Gaza proposal had been the "sole constructive measure" to be advocated in pursuit of a solution to the refugee problem. Not only that, but Abd al-Khaliq Hassuna was reported to be "hotly antagonistic to [the] Israeli desire [to] take possession [of] additional territory . . . and expressed surprise that US G[overnment] could regard such [a] measure as [a] constructive proposal."[25]

The secretary of state reacted to the reservations expressed in Cairo by reassuring the Egyptians that the US was not "insisting they agree to [the] Gaza strip proposal," only that they should not summarily dismiss it. The American government felt that the proposal "ha[d] merit" and believed it was "essential that it be discussed between [the] parties." Agreement to discuss was not, Acheson argued, a commitment to accept. Agreement to meet with the Israelis would be seen as a "concrete statesmanlike gesture," while outright refusal would leave Egypt open to accusations of bad faith and would "undoubtedly be used" by the Israelis as an "opportunity for [a] propaganda campaign."[26]

The American secretary also resumed his quest for Foreign Office support for the Gaza initiative, and responded to British reservations by stressing that "Egyptian agreement [to] enter into such discussions in no rpt no way prejudice[d] Egypt's ability to put forth... conditions" during (but not before) the talks. Acheson repeated that a categorical refusal by Egypt would "undoubtedly result in [the] charge that Egypt [was] obstructing progress toward [a] peace settlement."[27] But the Foreign Office remained reluctant to press the Egyptians on the Gaza proposal "in isolation from other points," particularly as such pressure might adversely affect the new package of British proposals which was then under consideration (see below).[28]

In the course of waiting for Egyptian assent, the nature of the proposed American involvement was altered. At first, Eban's talks at the State Department had left him optimistic that the Americans were offering not so much to "mediate" as to facilitate direct Israel-Egypt talks.[29] Indeed, at one point Acheson had informed the American ambassador to the United Nations that the US had no intention of "participat[ing] as [a] third party in [the] discussions or act[ing] as mediator"; if any mediation were required, Acheson wanted this to fall to the PCC.[30] But, as it became clear that diplomatic representations were not having the desired effect on Cairo's negative attitude to the proposal, the Americans felt forced to intervene more actively by offering to support Egyptian claims for territorial compensation. As we have seen, the possibility of Israel offering Egypt territorial compensation for Gaza had always been present in State Department (and especially Ethridge's) thinking, but this dimension became especially relevant when Americans were confronted by expressions of Egyptian distaste for Israel's Gaza proposal as being "straight barter of refugees against territory."[31] Such Egyptian arguments were seen, by some, not purely as humanitarian but also as tactical, reinforcing the view that a deal over Gaza might be possible if only a sufficiently large territorial *quid pro quo* could be obtained from Israel.[32]

Between 15 and 17 July, the American *chargé* in Cairo was hard at work under instructions to elicit an affirmative Egyptian reply through meetings with British and Egyptian officials. During his talk with Ambassador Sir Ronald Campbell, *Chargé* Patterson expressed himself as being

> anxious to make more clear to the Egyptians the American suggestion that if they gave up the Gaza Strip, the United States Government would give them diplomatic support for territorial compensation elsewhere. The idea was also to remove any idea that it was a question of exchange of territory against lives.

In addition to reviewing his previously expressed doubts about the Gaza proposal, the British ambassador pointed to the inability of Egyptian leaders to embark on such a risky foreign-policy venture on the eve of national elections. In conversation with Sir Ronald Campbell on 16 July, the Egyptian prime minister was reported to have "referred with some bitterness to the United States proposal for cession of the Gaza Strip to Israel."[33]

Patterson's report of his talks was even more colorful, describing a unanimous Egyptian reaction of "great... and... contemptuous surprise that the government of a great nation such as [the] US should lend itself to such [a] disreputable scheme." The American diplomat feared that the State Department's "continued harping on [the] merits of [the] Gaza plan" — which he described as "completely invisible to Arab eyes" — would cause the Egyptians to view the US government "as an accomplice of an expansionist and aggressive Israel." The American *chargé* had "never seen [Foreign] Minister [Khashaba] so violent in manner or so contemptuous of any proposal made to him."[34]

In another conversation reported by Patterson, Arab League Secretary-General Abd al-Rahman Azzam was less emotional in tone, but nevertheless criticized the US government for being "wittingly or unwittingly... (the) stooge or dupe of [the] Israelis who, according to his information, were preparing to attack Gaza... and to seize the area by force." Azzam could

> not perceive how [the] State Department (or he surmised the White House) could be so artless or so base as to lend itself to such an intrigue. The Zionist maneuver toward Gaza (part of an attempt to seize all of Palestine including Jerusalem) was so transparent that when it had been originally broached at Lausanne he had supposed that everyone would laugh the Israelis to scorn.

But now, Azzam mocked, the US government came along "and with a straight face support[ed] the proposal as being [the] sole possible solution of [the] refugee problem." Why, he asked, did the US not lend its support to the protocol of 12 May, instead of the "disreputable" Gaza scheme, which was "unworthy of consideration of any self-respecting government"?

But the fact that Jefferson Patterson ended his six-page report with the suggestion that "Egypt... might adopt [a] more conciliatory attitude towards [the] proposed settlement" if the State Department could "guarantee Egypt territorial compensation sufficient [to] provide [a] land bridge between Egypt [and] Jordan" may well have led Washington to interpret these expressions of indignation more as bargaining tactics than genuine moral outrage and rejection.[35] In hopes of winning Cairo's cooperation regarding the Gaza proposal, the Americans appeared prepared to support "reasonable" Egyptian territorial claims on the Negev.[36] But, in going this far, the US was exceeding the normal limits of providing good offices by undertaking to deliver goods which it really had no power to deliver. Indeed, an awareness that the Americans were contemplating backing Egyptian claims to the southern Negev may have been prominent among Foreign Minister Sharett's reasons for ordering a significant hardening of his Lausanne delegation's bargaining position after 25 July. In any possible discussions of the Gaza proposal, Israelis were told to reject out of hand any proposal for territorial compensation to Egypt and/or Jordan.[37]

The only possible bright spot in Patterson's lengthy report of 19 July was Abd al-Mun'im Mustafa's guarded concession to agree to discuss the Gaza proposal with the PCC on his return to Lausanne. But Egyptians would not, Mustafa affirmed, agree to do so at Lake Success, nor would he deal directly with Israeli delegates in Lausanne on the matter. Ultimately, the head of the Egyptian delegation predicted, he would reject the proposal as not being in accord with the protocol of 12 May, under which Gaza was defined as Arab territory. Clinging to the feeble straw held out by Abd al-Mun'im Mustafa, Secretary Acheson cabled the American delegation at Lausanne, suggesting that the PCC "take the initiative privately" to raise the Gaza question with the Egyptian delegate, and to offer to sound out the Israelis confidentially on the extent of the territorial concessions they would be prepared to make in exchange for Gaza.[38] But there was little reason for optimism at Lausanne. When approached by the Americans, Mustafa (contrary to assurances given in Cairo) rejected the Gaza proposal outright, while Reuven Shiloah (who replaced Eytan as head of the Israeli delegation) followed his instructions by not appearing overly eager to pursue the matter.[39]

On 25 July the long-awaited official Egyptian reply came as somewhat of an anticlimax. Egypt's formal rejection of the American proposal was prefaced by complaints about the inability of the powers to enforce compliance with the General Assembly resolution of 11 December 1948 regarding the right of the refugees to return to their homes. The Egyptian *aide-mémoire* regretted that international authorities were "docilely lending themselves to the game" being played by "the Jews." Egypt could "only refuse" the American proposal "which under humanitarian guise [could] serve only and solely the interests of the Jews who [were] merely making use of the refugee question as a means to extend their dominion over [the] largest part if not the entirety of Palestine."[40]

From Washington, the State Department informed its Cairo Embassy that, although it could not agree with the contentions in the Egyptian reply, it now believed it was "undesirable to continue to press [the] Egyptian government *re* Gaza strip proposal," and that the "proper focus of discussions [of] this subject" should be Lausanne.[41] In Washington, George McGhee informed Ambassador Elath that, while it had not proved possible to arrange for direct Egyptian-Israeli talks on the Gaza proposal during the PCC recess, he "hoped that future developments at Lausanne might lead to this result through a simultaneous discussion of such interlinked subjects as territory and refugees." Attempting to soften the impact of the Egyptian refusal, McGhee suggested that Egypt's "inability" to discuss the proposal was "not indicative of a lack of desire for peace[,] but was merely based on Arab emphasis on other matters such as repatriation under the GA Resolution of 11 December." The Israeli ambassador found this interpretation quite unconvincing, and reported McGhee as having been "embarrassed" by Egypt's attitude.[42]

In late July, after more than two months of negative signals from Cairo, Israeli and American officials finally put the Gaza plan — as a focus for direct Egyptian-Israeli negotiations or for American mediation — on hold. During the coming months, some officials continued to entertain the faint possibility of one day reviving Israel's offer to incorporate the strip and its refugees.[43] In the context of a renewed UK-Israeli diplomatic dialogue in August and the Foreign Office's promotion of its eight-point peace plan, the British attitude to the Gaza scheme appeared less categorically negative than in the past,[44] and the idea would later be revived as one ingredient in the ambitious Anglo-American Operation Alpha of 1955-56. But the Israelis were now clearly unwilling to consider any territorial compensation for Egypt or Jordan in the southern Negev. Israelis and Egyptians themselves soon realized, through secret talks in Lausanne in August, that their stands on the Negev were utterly irreconcilable.[45]

The British Eight-Point Plan

During the recess of the Lausanne talks, further steps were taken towards harmonizing American and British approaches and policies regarding the Palestine problem. A close look at the evidence would seem to contradict the view of one researcher that there was "massive British involvement in the proceedings in Lausanne." While there were certainly "regular meetings between British ministers and officials of the US, France and Turkey on the issues discussed at Lausanne," the degree of active British involvement can hardly be described as "massive."[46] It would be more accurate to describe the pattern of British involvement as one in which the Foreign Office was gingerly prodding a reluctant State Department, from the sidelines, towards a common approach. These British approaches enjoyed occasional encouragement from individual American officials.

The Americans were consistent, throughout 1949, in refusing to advance their own ideas for a solution, despite pressure to become actively involved coming from both British and Arab quarters. But the frustrating experience of two months of talks at Lausanne helped to create an apparent openness, among certain State Department officials, to the idea of the US playing a more active role in concert with the British government. When Raymond Hare visited London in early July to share his impressions of the recently-adjourned Lausanne conference, he provided an opportunity for increased Anglo-American cooperation with a view toward breaking the stalemated talks. Hare informed the Foreign Office that he expected that, upon the reconvening of discussions after 18 July, the PCC might be "asked by both sides to make proposals." Once British officials ascertained that the Americans "would be glad to receive any communication from us we might desire," the Foreign Office moved closer to the idea of submitting a set of proposals for joint Anglo-American action on resolving the Palestine *impasse*.[47] A direct suggestion for such a joint US-UK policy was made several days later in Sir William Strang's comprehensive report of his tour of Middle Eastern capitals.[48]

On 9 July, the Foreign Office prepared a "Suggested Basis for a New Approach by the Conciliation Commission to the Parties on their Resumption of Work on the 18th July."[49] The plan contained eight points:

1. acceptance by both sides of refugees "in proportions to be determined";
2. inclusion of Israel's proposal to incorporate the Gaza Strip as part of a general settlement, subject to adequate territorial compensation and the safeguarding of the rights and interests of Gaza refugees;
3. suggestions of areas considered "politically and geographically suitable" to be offered by Israel for territorial compensation, including "a land-bridge in the southern Negev between Egypt and Jordan";
4. provision of sea outlets for Arabs and Israelis to both the Red and Mediterranean Seas;
5. free port facilities for the Arab states in Haifa, including an arrangement for the resumption of the flow of Iraqi oil through that port;
6. partition of Jerusalem for administrative purposes, with international supervision of the Holy Places;
7. incorporation of Arab Palestine into Jordan; and
8. an Israeli-Arab agreement for sharing the waters of the Jordan and Yarmuk Rivers.

On 12 July, a slightly revised version of the eight-point outline was forwarded to Washington for comments. The next day, the State Department cabled its initial "informal" comments to London, where Michael Wright commented that American support for the British proposals would (unlike the ill-fated, single-issue American Gaza proposa) likely result in Arab and Israeli acceptance.[50] Discussions in

Washington and telegrams from London during the following weeks sought to clarify the proposals, with the British becoming impatient with the State Department's inability to go beyond the expression of its "tentative thinking" on most of the points. Meanwhile, British diplomats stationed in the Middle East were called upon to offer their comments on the suggested Eight Points.[51]

On 1 August, the US State Department reported "substantial agreement in principle" following continued consultations, and considered that the submission of the proposals to the PCC and the parties would be "most timely at this stage."[52] But the Foreign Office, in studying the latest American comments on the Eight Points, still felt handicapped without the State Department's "formal," rather than "informal" or "tentative," agreement in principle. From London, Ambassador Douglas recommended that his government take the initiative to begin discussing the plan with the French and Turkish governments, as a preliminary to the PCC presenting the plan to the Arab and Israeli delegations at Lausanne, "backed up by strong diplomatic support from [the] UK [and the] US."[53] In reply, Secretary Acheson offered additional comments on some of the Eight Points, but questioned the need for a formal US endorsement and considered it "preferable to maintain flexibility at this stage rather than to adopt [a] rigid position."[54]

Thus, it was with only lukewarm American support that the Foreign Office instructed its ambassadors in Paris and Ankara on 8 August to approach the French and Turkish governments with the details of the latest draft of the eight-point plan. Despite positive reactions to the Eight Points from French and Turkish authorities,[55] the plan did not, in the end, become integrated into the workings of the PCC. This appears to have been due mainly to the State Department's new orientation, in August 1949, to proceed with an "economic" — rather than a "political" — approach to solving the refugee issue. Still, the proposals served as a rough guide for evolving British policy on a Palestine settlement,[56] and constituted an important milestone in the quest for Anglo-American cooperation in the Middle East.

CHAPTER 9

Resumption of the Conference

The overall atmosphere at Lausanne following the break appeared more positive than before, although participants were still guarded about the chances of ultimate success. Without wishing to indulge in wishful thinking, the new head of the Israeli delegation, Reuven Shiloah, reacted positively to the improvement he detected in the attitude of the US delegation and to signs of moderation in the Arab position.[1] Until they were forced into silence by clarifications by the State Department, Israeli spokesmen played up signs of apparent American (especially presidential) approval or gratification at Israel's new bargaining stance on the refugee question.[2] The signing of the last remaining armistice agreement in the Israel-Syrian demilitarized zone on 20 July seemed to augur well for more fruitful negotiations at Lausanne. Following Syrian strongman Husni Za'im's extraordinary offer to resettle 300,000 (soon reduced to 200,000) Palestinian refugees in his country, Americans had reason to hope, for a short while, that the Syrian delegation might "facilitate [a] solution of [the] refugee problem" and use its influence to "induce other [Arab] del[egation]s to adopt [a] similar position simultaneously at Lausanne."[3] Israel was also interested in sending peace feelers towards Syria at this time.[4] Overall, both Arabs and Israelis "showed less intransigence" on their return to Lausanne, in large part due to the "internal" and "external" pressures that had operated during the recess.[5]

But there were also reasons for pessimism. In early conversations with Egypt's Abd al-Mun'im Mustafa and Israel's Gershon Hirsch, Stuart Rockwell of the American delegation found the two sides espousing the same mutually incompatible positions on refugees and territory. The only apparent improvement was the Egyptians' broadened mandate to discuss matters other than refugees. Rockwell also noted that the Arab states had been unable to come up with a common position of territorial issues during the recess.[6] Indeed, given the current notions of Israel being asked to make a trade-off between its conquered territories in Galilee and the Negev, it appeared that Syria's and Lebanon's interests would conflict with those of Egypt.[7] Within a few weeks, Israelis reported a turn for the worse in Egypt's attitude, while the Jordanians, owing partly to internal reasons, appeared more uncooperative and disillusioned after the recess than the other Arab delegations.[8] The mid-August visit to Lausanne of representatives of the All-Palestine Government in Gaza and a Gaza refugee organization was seen by some as an effort, through "advising" the Egyptian delegation, to subvert any chance of Arab-Israeli understanding or agreement.[9] Following the 14 August *coup d'état* which ousted and executed Husni Za'im, the Syrian line on cooperation with the US and the PCC noticeably hardened.[10]

On the Israeli side too, apparent signs of new flexibility or optimism were undermined by several factors. Reuven Shiloah's private conversations with Paul Porter led the former to believe that he had won the American representative over to the view that Israel's position was essentially "logical and justified"; hence Shiloah believed there would be no need for Israel to fear further pressure from Washington, and no need to contemplate further compromises at Lausanne.[11] Paradoxically, the conclusion of the final GAA with Syria — which might have produced added momentum towards a comprehensive settlement at Lausanne — led some Israelis instead to question the urgency of achieving a formal peace at this stage. Now that there was calm along the borders, and now that the cease-fire lines were acquiring a certain measure of international legitimacy as armistice lines, an imperceptible but important shift took place in the thinking of many Israeli policy makers regarding the need for a peace agreement at this time. In mid-July, David Ben-Gurion confided to journalist Kenneth Bilby that he had no faith in the

Lausanne conference ("A man like Bunche might have succeeded"): "even though I am ready to get up in the middle of the night to sign a peace [accord], I am not in a hurry and am prepared to wait ten years. We are under no pressure."[12] This change of emphasis affected not only "hard liners" and skeptics, but also men like Sharett, Sasson, and Eban, who were normally committed to exerting maximum efforts to reach a satisfactory agreement with the Arab states at Lausanne. The prime minister quoted Eban approvingly, to the effect that there was no need to "chase after peace"; an armistice was "sufficient for us. If we chase after peace, the Arabs will demand a price from us — borders or refugees or both. Let us wait a few years."[13] A consensus was developing in the Ministry of Foreign Affairs that Israel should

> stop reiterating declarations about our desire for peace, since the Arab world interprets them as a sign of weakness and as an indication of our willingness to surrender. We should say the opposite [Sharett lectured his Mapai party colleagues]: We do not need peace. We are satisfied with the present agreement. Perhaps the Arabs need peace.[14]

Although such cavalier attitudes were not overtly displayed by the Israeli delegation at Lausanne, they certainly operated as an undercurrent to the ongoing diplomatic maneuvering and posturing of the Israeli delegation. Upon his arrival at Lausanne on 27 July, Reuven Shiloah informally advised Paul Porter about an important tactical retreat in his country's position — a change which Shiloah attributed to the latest manifestations of US pressure.[15] Israel was, he said, now prepared to discuss solutions to the refugee problem "outside [the] context of [a] final Palestine settlement," so long as there was convincing evidence that "real progress" was being made toward such a "final settlement." The long-standing Israeli linkage between a refugee settlement and an overall peace agreement was now broken. On territory, however, Shiloah made it clear that the PCC would have a "bitter wrangle" with the Israeli delegation over any plans involving a reduction of territory currently occupied by Israel. Israel "might," Porter reported in quotation marks, consider suggestions for territorial "adjustments" which did not involve loss of the Negev. The American delegate was "not encouraged" by what he had heard.[16]

Several days later, the Israeli position on the refugee problem was submitted in writing, and contained the additional condition that discussions on the issue "must be held directly between Israeli and Arab delegates in [the] presence of [the] PCC."[17] After several days of confusing signals, the Arab delegations confirmed that they were willing to discuss the Israeli proposals with the commission, but that face-to-face discussions with the Israelis were "out of the question."[18] During a meeting with the PCC on 3 August, the Israeli delegation formally announced that the number of refugees Israel would allow to return would be set at 100,000.[19]

Israel's Offer to Repatriate 100,000 Refugees

The government of Israel had decided on the figure of 100,000 during the Lausanne recess, in response to repeated and persistent requests from the PCC and the US government for a commitment to the number of refugees it would be willing to repatriate. Informal soundings had been made as to the likely reactions from Washington, and consultations held on the optimum manner and timing of the proposed announcement.[20] On 28 July, the president and the State Department were advised of the imminent Israeli offer before it was presented to the PCC at Lausanne. Moshe Sharett also chose this issue as the one with which to break the ice and test Ernest Bevin's recent declarations of friendship to Israel; a confidential appeal was made to the Foreign Office to use its influence in helping to gain a positive Arab response to the 100,000 offer.[21]

As a negotiating position, the 100,000 offer had little success in winning American favor in moving the Lausanne talks forward. The very fact that Israel had offered to incorporate the Gaza Strip — whose refugee population was variously estimated at between 150,000 and 250,000 — became a liability to the current Israeli negotiating position, making the 100,000 offer seem a paltry token by comparison. Some American officials, like Consul-General William Burdett in Jerusalem, were openly hostile and cynical, believing that Israel had "no intention whatsoever" [to] conform with UNGA resolution 194 "in either letter or spirit," and that the family reunion and 100,000 offers "possess[ed] many earmarks of [a] sham to evade efforts [of the] US and UN."[22] Secretary of State Acheson noted that, "on balance," the US did not consider the Israeli offer to be a "satisfactory ... basis for [an] ultimate solution of [the] refugee problem."[23] Most American officials, as well as the Foreign Office, regarded the 100,000 as a constructive first step — but one that would need to be improved upon.[24] Despite the lukewarm international response and the fact that it did not result in breaking the Lausanne deadlock, Foreign Minister Sharett nevertheless believed that the offer had "vastly improved" Israel's "tactical position" *vis-à-vis* the UN and the Arabs.[25]

The "100,000 offer" — which historian Benny Morris places in quotation marks and shows to have amounted to less, in fact, than 100,000[26] — became further undermined when a press leak unleashed "a major political explosion in Tel Aviv." Hostile criticism of the government's offer, even within Mapai party ranks, reflected (a) security fears of the reintroduction of a "fifth column," (b) fears that Israel would be forced beyond the 100,000 to allow the return of larger numbers, (c) distaste for the apparent surrender to US pressure, and (d) a popular backlash against the return of any of the refugees. Foreign Minister Sharett pointed to this internal opposition to reinforce the point that 100,000 was the absolute maximum Israel would consider. In the circumstances, the offer was truly being made on a "take-it-or-leave-it" basis.[27]

At first the PCC decided not to transmit the new Israeli offer on the refugee problem formally to the Arab delegations, "since if it did so instant rejection would result and [an] *impasse* [would] be created." Private talks between commissioners and Arab delegates revealed an "emphatic" rejection of Israel's offer as a "mere propaganda scheme" and "less than token." At a subsequent private meeting with Shiloah, PCC members attempted, in vain, to get the Israelis to improve on their offer — leaving Porter convinced that "although [the] atmosphere may appear more conciliatory on [the] surface[,] basic positions remain unchanged."[28] The Arab delegations denounced the inadequacy of the Israeli offer on refugees, and referred again to the protocol of 12 May as the basis for their request for an immediate return of refugees to Israeli-held lands lying outside the 1947 partition boundaries. Rockwell found this counterproposal so "unrealistic and unhelpful" that he decided not to forward it to the Israelis.[29]

From Washington, the American government tried again to induce Israeli "flexibility," this time by suspending payment of the unallocated balance of a $100 million loan previously granted by the Export-Import (ExIm) Bank of Washington, citing the non-realization of anticipated peace in Palestine. The idea of applying this financial "stick" against Israel had first been proposed by the State Department as a possible follow-up to Truman's 29 May note of rebuke and had been endorsed by the president after mid-July. While the State Department refused to admit to the Israeli ambassador that it was exerting any political veto in the loan matter, this is the clear message which the Israelis drew (and were expected to draw) from both the ExIm Bank itself and from Stuart Rockwell in Lausanne. The latter had been taking a "strong line" in his talks with Israeli representatives on the "unlikelihood... of large scale US-Israel economic cooperation [in] view [of the] Israeli attitude on [the] main issues [of the] Palestine problem."[30]

Perhaps because of poor timing and confusing political signals sent to Israeli representatives, the suspension (or "postponement," as McGhee apologetically termed it) of the loan payments had no impact on the 100,000 offer. As in the case of John Foster Dulles' October 1953 suspension of American aid in an attempt to coerce Israel into stopping work on the Benot Yaakov water-diversion project, the 1949 suspension illustrated the limited effects of great-power sanctions on embattled client-states.[31] If anything, the American action had the opposite effect of sparking Israel's outrage and determination, especially when coupled with the latter's frustration at the lack of US understanding shown towards the Gaza and 100,000 offers.[32]

If the Americans were hoping to change Israel's position by the loan suspension, Sharett warned, they were "mistaken in their estimation of our moral and physical capacity to stand firm." The Israeli foreign minister added that, since the Arabs were hoping for Israel's economic ruin, the American move would also encourage extremists and put off the chances of peace.[33] In late August, the Israelis mounted a counteroffensive behind closed doors, requesting a reconsideration and threatening that, if the matter became public, they would denounce the political interference as a breach of faith hindering Israel's economic consolidation. During a meeting with George McGhee, Ambassador Elath called it the "worst blow we ever suffered" at the hands of the American government, and hoped the reversal of the State Department veto would become a "turning point to force [an] improvement [in] our relations and compel [the] USA government [to] relinquish [its] methods [of] coercion and blackmail."[34] The Israelis were pleased when the State Department finally backed away from its attempt to use the loan payments as political leverage at Lausanne, but the Arabs were left with the impression that US support of UNGA resolutions and the "reported American threats against Israel" were merely "empty talk."[35]

CHAPTER 10

Continued Conciliation or Imposed Settlement?

On the major issues of refugees and territories, the parties were once again at an *impasse*. Nor was there any thaw or increase in goodwill resulting from attempts to resolve ostensibly minor or technical matters. Israel's proposed practical arrangements for the reunification of refugee families, modest though they were, led to a delayed, begrudging and conditional Arab response — producing, in turn, bitter complaints from Israelis both in Lausanne and Tel Aviv.[1] A precedent for direct Arab-Israeli official meetings was set when the Arab delegations agreed to the creation of a mixed technical committee to study the implementation of an accord on the unblocking of frozen bank accounts, but bureaucratic and political difficulties prevented this subcommittee from showing any concrete results for several years.[2]

By mid-August, it appeared that the latest stalemate in the Lausanne talks might be broken in one of two ways. Either the PCC would transmit its own set of proposals to the delegations for discussion, and thereafter continue (indirect) negotiations on this new basis; or the commission would adjourn the talks, and report to the UNGA on the failure of the parties to reach agreement at Lausanne. This report would conceivably provide the Assembly with recommendations for an equitable solution.

Pressure for the first course came chiefly from Paul Porter, and was directed at the State Department. After only one week at the resumed talks, the dejected head of the American delegation had informed Secretary Acheson that there were "no grounds for optimism," as the parties were "apparently... willing to continue endless and aimless discussions." He had suggested to his PCC colleagues that, if no agreement were to emerge after two more weeks of talks, the commission itself should then be prepared to "initiate proposals that in its view [were] equitable." He requested State Department advice on the recommended lines of a settlement, and urged the need to have a well-formulated position ready for presentation.[3]

While concurring in Porter's idea of a self-imposed two-week deadline, Acheson instructed the Lausanne delegation to avoid "anything in the nature of a PCC plan" until at least after a further stage during which the commissioners would informally advance tentative, *ad hoc* practical suggestions for discussion.[4] Despite the requests from Lausanne and despite the availability of the FO's Eight Points as a potential basis for a settlement, the State Department seemed intent on sticking to its cautious, noninterventionist approach. Much had happened during the past six months to render inoperative the State Department's January instructions which had promised Mark Ethridge recourse to either the Jessup principle or an agreed Anglo-American approach when needed to break the *impasse* in the conciliation effort.

At Lausanne, however, the members of the commission began the process of formulating their own preliminary proposals for territorial compromises, with the French, Turkish and American representatives pulling in different directions and reflecting the different sensitivities of their respective governments. On 5 August, Paul Porter pressed for State Department approval to have the commission proceed to elaborate those tentative proposals in private meetings with each delegation.[5] Recognizing differences within the commission itself and some divergences from the existing American position on territorial adjustments, Acheson again warned his Lausanne delegation against attempting to hammer out a single PCC position. The secretary preferred the PCC to seek agreement on "various alternative plans as [a] basis for possible discussion between the parties" and pointed out that the delegation's territorial proposals were "at considerable variance with [the] position [the] US has previously taken," and hence should not be advanced as "final" or "official" American policy.[6] It was perhaps during this brief interlude of Porter's tentative quest for a PCC package of proposals that the Arab delegations reported the appearance of an attractive eight-point "American plan" which left the Israeli delegates "outraged."[7]

Several days later, during a closed PCC meeting, Porter was reported to have argued in favor of the commission leaving Lausanne and reconvening in New York in order to prepare its report for the General Assembly. Israeli delegates also gained the impression that Porter was considering returning to Washington to offer his resignation, "depressed and convinced that he could do nothing more at Lausanne" and believing that the time had come for vigorous American intervention at the United Nations.[8]

The prospect that the Palestine question would be placed on the agenda of the September UNGA soon became a factor which complicated and overshadowed the resumed Lausanne discussions. The Americans hoped that the fear of being blamed before the Assembly for the failure of the conference would have a salutary effect on all delegations by inducing greater flexibility and a commitment to the success of the negotiations.[9] But this was not necessarily the effect on the Arab delegations. Ever since the Beirut conference of March, Arab representatives had been dismayed by the noncommittal attitude adopted by the commissioners.[10] In August, most Arab delegates were still hoping that the Lausanne meetings would (a) work out the ways and means for implementing the 1947 partition boundaries and/or (b) reaffirm the December 1948 resolution regarding the return of Palestinian refugees. The new "threat" that the PCC might call upon the General Assembly to adopt new resolutions imposing a solution along these lines was, to most Arab delegates, no threat at all, but precisely what they had been demanding.[11] Hence, all talk about winding up the conference and reporting to the UNGA amounted to a disincentive for the Arabs to try to achieve any of their goals through greater flexibility at Lausanne.

The Israeli delegation had been hoping to avoid, at all costs, a debate in the UNGA. In attempting to deflect such an outcome, Reuven Shiloah protested that it would be "unwise for [the] PCC to deal with

[the] important problems involved in [a] Palestine settlement in [a] hurried atmosphere of working against [the] G[eneral] A[ssembly] deadline." Israel, he affirmed, would not be pressured into concessions by anyone brandishing the threat of the forthcoming Assembly. American maneuvers in this direction, he warned, would only lead Arabs and Israelis to concentrate on preparing their cases rather than negotiating the issues at Lausanne.[12] From the UN, Abba Eban advised the Lausanne delegation to "sell" the PCC the advantages of continuing the talks even during the fall General Assembly session, while he himself lobbied against an imposed settlement and in favor of keeping the Assembly committed to its earlier resolutions based on the principle of allowing the parties to settle their disputes "by negotiation and agreement."[13]

There was a particular American angle to Israeli fears of a debate in the UNGA. In early June, Eban in New York had warned Eytan in Lausanne that the State Department's reiteration of the Jessup principle might tempt the commission "to turn aside from mediating [*sic*, for conciliating or facilitating] functions in order to adopt a policy of reviving Bernadottism" — i.e., full "mediation" including the formal submission of proposals unacceptable to Israel.[14] Two months later, Eytan (now returned to Tel Aviv) predicted that the US was about to present a "prefabricated proposal" to the PCC, which would then be "impose[d] upon the Arabs and ourselves," with subsequently "practically one hundred percent certainty of acceptance by the General Assembly whether the Arabs and we like it or not." In sketching out the likely lines of such an imposed settlement, Eytan speculated that it would end up being "thoroughly acceptable to the Arabs, though of course they will do a good deal of gesticulating and grumbling for form's sake."

> I have also no doubt that a scheme of this sort would be thoroughly unacceptable to us, and that we could never under any circumstances agree to it. That being so, we should be in a very difficult position indeed at the forthcoming General Assembly, with the Arabs appearing as moderate and reasonable beings, while we shall be traditionally stiff-necked.[15]

Before long, Shiloah and the Israeli delegation seemed to detect, in their contacts with members of the American delegation, the prospect of the very scenario that Eytan had warned about. Others at Lausanne, including Claude de Boisanger and the head of the Egyptian delegation, also suspected (incorrectly) that the Americans were maneuvering for an opportunity to impose their own ideas for a settlement *via* the UNGA.[16] Even later, when the PCC had dissolved the Lausanne conference, Sasson did not believe that US pressure for a "Jessup formula" territorial arrangement would abate.[17]

The principal parties took diametrically opposed positions on the very idea of the PCC submitting its own proposals. The Israelis had reacted negatively when they first began to suspect that the PCC was considering such a course.[18] In late July, when the prospect seemed more likely, Abba Eban advised the Lausanne delegation that

> whenever a territorial proposal is made we should enquire from which Arab States [*sic*] it comes and express readiness to discuss it directly with that Arab State. After all[,] we are not discussing our common frontiers with the US, France or Turkey [members of the PCC], and nothing could be more futile than to think of territorial adjustments outside the framework of direct Arab-Jewish negotiations.[19]

The American ambassador in Tel Aviv supported the Israeli position on the inappropriateness of the commission proposing a territorial solution, warning that any PCC initiative, especially contemplated territorial compromises, would be futile and perhaps even dangerous.[20] Likewise, the French member of the PCC, Claude de Boisanger, dissented from his American and Turkish colleagues in Lausanne, claiming that their mandate was to "conciliate" but not to "arbitrate."[21] What Israelis really feared was that, through the medium of the PCC, the parties might be forced to accept the US position on territorial arrangements, which continued to be, throughout 1949, essentially the "Jessup principle" enunciated in late 1948:

> If Israel wishes to retain any areas in Palestine allocated to the proposed Arab state under the UN resolution of 29 November 1947

> and now occupied by Israeli forces, Israel should, if the Arab states so demand, make territorial compensation elsewhere and/or make other concessions of a non-territorial character as are required to reach an equitable agreement which could provide the basis for a lasting peace.[22]

Israeli spokesmen devoted their efforts to avoiding the implementation of this US position, which would have required Israel to give up part of the Negev in exchange for lands conquered in Galilee beyond the 1947 partition lines.[23]

Although members of the Lebanese and Egyptian delegations indicated, during informal conversations, that they were in favor of the continuation of the Lausanne conference,[24] a number of Arab spokesmen appeared eager at this time to invite outside intervention. Lebanon's minister in Washington, Charles Malik, went so far as to suggest that the Americans, French and British (rather than the PCC) take time out immediately to devise — and impose, with "firm political guidance" — a durable peace plan on the Middle East.[25] This was consistent with earlier expressions by Arab leaders of the view that, given the impossibility of them ever contemplating direct negotiations and an agreement which would recognize Israel, and given the prospect that the Jewish state was "here to stay," the only solution possible would be one imposed by Britain and America.[26] In mid-August, the Foreign Office received signals, *via* the Turkish representative on the PCC, that the

> Arab governments were anxious to reach a solution for Palestine as soon as possible, but that owing to the state of public opinion in Middle East countries and to other difficulties they could not put forward a solution themselves.... they would probably accept a reasonable solution if it were imposed on them by the United Nations. They therefore hoped that the United Nations would take the initiative.[27]

Egypt, in particular, declared itself eager for a speedy resolution of the Palestine problem, and its UN delegate indicated privately that his government would accept "reasonable proposals" if they came from the UN, rather than Israel. Mahmud Fawzi hoped the

PCC would direct the talks by sounding out the parties on its own proposals.[28] Direct, secret Egyptian-Israeli contacts in Lausanne, which disclosed absolute deadlock over claims to the Negev, had the effect of reinforcing this Egyptian inclination to hope for a settlement imposed by the UNGA.[29]

On 11 August, Abba Eban offered an elaborate defense of the continuation of the conciliation effort and argued forcefully against the use of the General Assembly to impose a settlement.[30] The Israeli representative at the UN glowingly endorsed the conclusion of Ralph Bunche's recent report on the armistice agreements between Israel and its neighbors,[31] to the effect that "once the parties could be brought together they could reach an honorable agreement." Israel's informal contacts with Arab delegates, he claimed, revealed no signs of "despair of a negotiated agreement," even though Arab spokesmen might be claiming publicly that it was difficult for them to conclude an agreement in the immediate future. If the Lausanne talks should fail, Israel's view was that this would be "due not to any impossibility of reaching an agreement between the parties, but to the circumstances surrounding this particular conciliation effort." At this point Eban detailed some of the questions which would be raised during the course of a possible United Nations "inquest" into the demise of the conciliation effort, focusing on the failings of the PCC itself. As "illuminating" as such an inquest would be, Israel would find it more desirable to persist in "obstinate and tenacious" efforts towards an agreement.

Basing himself on the fifth paragraph of the much-invoked UNGA resolution 194 of 11 December 1948, Eban went on to warn against attempts of the Assembly to dictate terms of a territorial settlement which really ought to be arrived at through negotiation. He argued that "to abandon conciliation would lead us into a far worse atmosphere than to continue it, even in the present difficult situation." Eban concluded by urging that the 20 September opening date for the General Assembly should not serve as an arbitrary and harmful deadline to the Lausanne talks. In summarizing the above arguments for the benefit of Eliahu Elath in Washington, Eban stressed that the question of a final territorial settlement was

> important but certainly not urgent in terms of weeks. The world will not come to an end if this question is not fully settled by the forthcoming Assembly.... The Governments directly concerned cannot be pushed or jostled by outside factors either into premature agreement, or what is more important, into premature conclusion of chronic disagreement.

Since the present situation was "not one of warfare or imminent violence, USA and UN policy [did] not have to keep on restlessly forcing the pace."[32] With the passage of UNSC resolution no. 73 (1949) on 11 August, Eban felt the Israeli position on continuing to seek an agreement by negotiation was vindicated. He would use the resolution in continuing his lobbying against the prospect of the adjournment of the Lausanne talks and an imposed settlement.[33]

CHAPTER 11

Winding up the Conference: The PCC Questionnaire and the Economic Survey Mission

Following up on one of Paul Porter's suggestions, and with endorsement of the US State Department, the PCC on 15 August presented each delegation with a memorandum which consisted of a summary of what had been achieved thus far, followed by a brief questionnaire soliciting more specific details on the positions of the parties regarding refugees and a territorial settlement.[1] The delegations were asked to respond within eight days, and US representative Rockwell cabled the State Department, asking it to make the appropriate representations to the Israeli and Arab governments in the quest for helpful replies.[2]

Meanwhile, on the basis of consultations with Ethridge and Porter in Washington, the State Department had reached its own clear-cut conclusions on the usefulness of prolonging the Lausanne talks:

> [N]o real basis for conciliation between the parties exist[ed] at the present time.... Although both sides w[ou]ld welcome peace, neither side is prepared at this time to make concessions which w[ou]ld make [a] settlement possible. Israeli offers *re* Gaza Strip or repatriation [of] 100,000 Arab refugees are unacceptable to [the] Arabs. [The] Arab position which is based on [a] rigid adherence to para[graph] 11 of GA res[olution] [of] Dec 11 [1948] and [the] May 12 protocol with its map indicating [the] 1947 partition boundaries is unacceptable to [the] Israelis.

Given the political *impasse*, the department wished to reorient its policies and procedures to reflect an economic approach. The key element of the new approach, inspired by the State Department's George McGhee, was the placing of the Palestinian refugee problem in the context of a "Marshall Plan" for the Middle East; the preparation of such a plan was assigned to the long-discussed Economic Survey Mission (ESM), which would shortly begin examining practical possibilities for refugee resettlement in the region. The report and recommendations of the ESM were expected by November, and would "cover all possible aspects of [the] Palestine question on econ[omic] grounds."[3]

With this in mind, Paul Porter visited senior French officials in Paris to persuade them that the Lausanne talks should be wound up without unnecessary delay.[4] The State Department proceeded to sound out the views of American diplomats in the region on the prospects of obtaining an advance commitment from the governments to which they were accredited to cooperate in the work of the ESM. Besides shifting the emphasis from political deadlock over formulas to practical arrangements and economic inducements, Porter felt personally that the work of the ESM would also provide a means by which to "let the dust settle."[5] The Israelis were already naturally predisposed to welcome the new approach, with Shiloah feeling confident that the Arab states' dependency on the US for development assistance would help convince them of the advantages of accepting refugee rehabilitation schemes. The head of the Israeli delegation went so far as to believe that the Arabs would "acquiesce in any settlement firmly advocated by the Americans even if it should entail coming to terms with the present territorial situation and absorbing the majority of the Arab refugees."[6]

But the usually perceptive Israeli official was seriously misjudging the mood in Arab capitals in late 1949. The American Embassy in Beirut endorsed the new emphasis on the economic approach, but warned against leaving the impression in the Arab world that the US and the PCC had been thwarted in Lausanne, and were now trying to hide this by launching yet another commission. The Lebanese foreign minister was reported expressing "greatest reservation concerning [the ESM's] usefulness and considerable skepticism as to its true objectives," which were suspected of being to relieve the desperate economic situation in Israel and to "force [the Arabs] into economic cooperation with Israel."[7] William Burdett in Jerusalem added his own doubts as to whether the ESM would meet with Arab approval to the extent that it appeared to accept the political *status quo*, which was viewed as favorable to Israel.[8] Likewise, the FO in London expressed its concern lest the new economic orientation allow the "present territorial situation to freeze." The American ambassador in London agreed, recommending that Washington "not relax [the] pressure for [a] political settlement."[9] On 24 August, Gordon R. Clapp was appointed to head the ESM, and on 1 September the mission's terms of reference were published at the United Nations.[10]

On 26 August, the commission announced its decision to bring the conference to a close by 15 September and to make use of the delegations' replies to the questionnaire in formulating its report to the UNGA.[11] At Lausanne, those wishing to see the continuation of the talks — rather than a debate at the UNGA — were well aware that much would depend on their replies to the questionnaire being perceived as conciliatory and helpful.[12] Although relations between the US and Israeli delegations had seemed to be taking a noticeable turn for the better, the Israelis were continuing to display, in the words of the American *chargé d'affaires* in Tel Aviv, their "ironclad determination... not to surrender any of the territory now physically occupied.... [I]t would be misleading and perhaps even dangerous to assume that Israel will give up any appreciable part of the territory which it now considers its own either by right of conquest or otherwise."[13] The Arab states replied to the PCC questionnaire with a lengthy but noncommittal memorandum which was based heavily on the partition resolution of 29 November 1947 and the protocol of 12 May 1949. Despite the stress on these common bases, the memorandum could not hide the fact that there were real differences among the various states regarding both territory and refugees. While Jordan was satisfied with the present boundaries, Syrian and Lebanon claimed parts of Galilee while the Egyptians called for the inclusion of the Negev in its territory. Syria and Jordan were willing to admit some of the refugees, while Egypt and Lebanon claimed that economic hardship made it impossible for them to accept any.[14] To the chagrin of the Arab delegations (who tried to prevent it), a separate reply was submitted by representatives of the Palestinian refugees.[15] On 31 August, Reuven Shiloah submitted Israel's official reply to the PCC questionnaire, which was nothing more than a reformulation of previously announced positions.[16]

In his reports to Washington, Stuart Rockwell, acting head of the American delegation, played up the positive which he found in the delegations' responses on the refugee question, describing the replies "fairly satisfactory in [the] circumstances." All delegations, notwithstanding their reservations, had committed themselves to facilitate the work of the Economic Survey Mission. Despite conflicting interpretations and disagreements between the Arab states and Israel, Rockwell believed that their replies could be "considered as [a] political agreement on sharing responsibility for [a] solution [to the] refugee problem."[17] On 5 September, the PCC informed the delegations of its intention to resume discussions in New York in late October. The commission now requested the delegations to sign a draft declaration regarding the refugee question embodying what it felt was the minimal consensus which had been achieved through the questionnaire responses: notably, that "[t]he solution to the refugee problem should be sought in the repatriation of refugees in Israeli-controlled territory *and* [my emphasis, N.C.] in the resettlement of those refugees not repatriated in such areas of Palestine as may be under Arab control, or in Arab countries." The PCC announced that it would submit, after further study, another set of proposals aimed at narrowing the gap between the two sides on the territorial issue.[18]

As was half-expected by the American delegation at Lausanne, the Arabs and Israelis indicated that that they would be unlikely to sign the proposed declaration on the refugee issue. The Arabs cited "public opinion at home" and the fact that the declaration "mention[ed] concessions they ha[d] made *re* refugees without reference to their territorial position." The Israelis were reported to be objecting to the implication that they accepted the declaration's premise that Lebanon and Egypt were not in a position to accept large numbers of refugees.[19]

It was, in Rockwell's view, the "wide divergence" in the parties' stands on the territorial question which "once more reveal[ed the] unlikelihood [of] arriving at [a] voluntary agreement." While he described the latest statement of the Arab states' position as "unreasonable" and weakened by a conflicting mixture of motives, the American representative dwelt on the "rigidity [of the] Israeli position." He saw no hope in "proceeding from [the] present armed truce line to more stable conditions unless Israel [could] be persuaded to relinquish some of [the] territory it has occupied beyond [the] partition lines." While he saw some "measure of agreement" on the refugee issue, Rockwell felt that the Arabs would "not accept any territorial solution which makes the armistice lines, perhaps with minor modifications, the final boundaries of Israel."[20]

On 8 September, the State Department urged its representative on the PCC to bring the Lausanne talks to a close as soon as possible, partly as a means of giving added emphasis to the importance of the ESM but also in the belief that prolonging the conference unduly would "result in [a] further hardening of [the] positions of [the] del[egation]s."[21] Those, like Eytan and de Boisanger, who suspected that the Americans were looking for an opportunity to bring the matter before the UNGA so as to impose a settlement were forced to recognize that the delegations' replies on the territorial issue, together with their refusal to sign the proposed declaration on refugees, had now provided Washington with the required pretext. As an expression of his dissatisfaction with the current maneuvers which pointed to an imposed settlement at the UN, Eliahu Sasson announced to members of the PCC that he, personally, would not be representing Israel at the proposed continuation of talks in New York. While Israel-Arab relations could only deteriorate if the issue were placed on the UNGA agenda, Sasson felt that a resumption of the PCC talks after receipt of the ESM report held out the prospect of more "constructive" talks and a reduction in the "extremism" of the Arab position. The Israeli delegate suggested that it was in Israel's interest to delay the reconvening of the talks for as long as possible.[22]

The final act of the PCC at the Lausanne conference came in the form of a memorandum addressed to each of the delegations on 12 September, consisting of the commission's critical observations on their replies to the questionnaire of 15 August. Among its comments on the Israeli position on the refugees, the PCC felt "bound to note" that the Israeli view on resettlement of the majority outside of Israel was "not in conformity with the terms of paragraph 11 of the General Assembly's resolution of 11 December 1948." A detailed consideration of numbers would best be left until after the report of the ESM. On the territorial issue, the commission announced its conclusion that Israel's demands "exceed[ed]" the negotiation of "adjustments," even "in the broadest sense," to the partition map which was the agreed "basis for discussion" in the protocol signed by all parties on 12 May. It asked the Israeli government to reexamine the question with a view to presenting a new proposal during the renewed talks in New York. The note concluded by urging that "no excessive territorial demands should be allowed to impede the realization" of the restoration of "normal conditions of political and economic life... at the earliest possible moment in the Middle East."[23]

The State Department consulted with Paris and Ankara regarding representations to be made to Israeli and Arab governments in order to "emphasize [the] importance attached to" their submission "of more flexible and reasonable proposals on territory" to the PCC in New York. But Acheson felt that these approaches should be "postpone[d]... for [the] moment" so as not to encumber the work of the ESM by the "injection [of] political questions."[24] The waiting period for the report of the ESM had the effect of granting Israel "precious time and a break from the American pressure" — pressure which (some have implied) might have resulted in Israeli concessions on refugees or territory and a last-minute breakthrough to a settlement.[25] Meanwhile the PCC submitted its Progress Report to the UN, expressing the hope that it would receive Arab and Israeli replies to its note of 12 September "which will be of a nature to permit the successful pursuit of its efforts to conciliate the points of view of the parties."[26] Instead of discussing how best to draft the memorandum requested by the commission for its New York session scheduled for 19 October, Israeli officials began considering not only how best to avoid attending that meeting, but also the possibility of launching an all-out campaign for the dissolution of the PCC.[27]

CHAPTER 12

Lausanne Postscripts

New York Meetings

By October 1949, the movement towards a general settlement which had motivated the Lausanne talks appeared to have fizzled out. As Secretary Acheson reported to US diplomatic missions, the positions of the parties in the wake of the Lausanne meetings remained "too far apart to offer hope [of a] definitive settlement [in the] foreseeable future, or even hope of producing [an] area of agreement on which [a] final settlement might be based." The scheduled meeting in New York was, in the State Department analysis, "not expected to produce any material improvement in conciliation." Acheson rightly noted that the *impasse* was "aggravated by [the] apparent conviction [of] each side that time work[ed] to its advantage," but American envoys were asked to point out to Middle Eastern governments the detrimental long-term effects of their current unyielding attitudes.[1] On 19 October, the commissioners met in New York without Arab or Israeli delegations, with whom it was decided to hold *pro forma* meetings "in the near future." It was felt that no useful meetings could be held until after receipt of the ESM report. Meanwhile, President Truman appointed Ely Palmer as US representative, replacing Paul Porter whose resignation had been received on 15 September.[2]

The greatest part of the attention and energy of the PCC in the fall of 1949 was diverted from the attempts at a comprehensive settlement to defending its proposals for an international regime for Jerusalem, a complicated subject which lies beyond the scope of the present study.[3] It remained, however, for the parties to issue their last word in reply to the PCC Note of 12 September. On 22 October, Fawzi al-Mulqi declared that the commission "must consider the present stand of the Arab delegations as their final one, beyond which they could not go until the commission itself presented suggestions or proposals." This "invitation" would be taken up by the PCC two years later, in Paris.[4] Meanwhile, the Arab delegations, led by Egypt's Abd al-Mun'im Mustafa, met with the commissioners on 24 October to complain about the still unfulfilled December 1948 UNGA resolution on the return of Palestinian refugees. The delegates refused to sign a PCC draft declaration regarding holy places outside Jerusalem, apparently in protest against the lack of progress on more important issues. The Egyptians proposed to submit a draft declaration on the rights of Arabs in Israeli-occupied territory for the commission's consideration and transmission to the Israelis.[5]

Israel delayed its official response to the PCC's final Lausanne note until 27 October. A week earlier, Ambassador Eban felt that the time was ripe for active lobbying in favor of eliminating UN conciliation agencies altogether, recommending that Israel adopt the following line: an affirmation of willingness to make peace with the Arabs, while pointing to the "political [and] psychological impossibility thereof if they will not meet" face-to-face. He also suggested that Israeli spokesmen "develop [the] theory [that] time and life may bring reconciliation."[6] In his formal reply to PCC chairman Yalçin, Eban repeated his government's stand on refugees — namely, that, apart from the family reunification scheme recently under way, "the question of Israel's contribution to the resettlement of the refugees can only arise in the context of a general peace settlement and as part of a comprehensive and final solution of the whole refugee problem." The ambassador rejected the commission's call to "reexamine" its position on territories as "neither equitable nor realistic, and... not based on a correct application or interpretation of the Protocol of May 12, 1949." Eban offered the first of several *post facto* clarifications of Israel's interpretation of the Lausanne Protocol, noting that:

That document was accepted by the delegation of Israel merely

> as a procedural device for canalizing the discussion and helping the Commission to make some practical start with its conciliation efforts. The Protocol in no way committed the Government of Israel to a reversion to the boundaries of the Jewish State as defined in the General Assembly's resolution of 29 November 1947.[7]

For some time afterward, the commission would continue to dispute this interpretation of Israel's "reserving" of its position.[8]

Eban went on to denounce the "selective validity" that Israel's critics were reading into the partition resolution, and went on to list some of its "basic assumptions" that had not materialized. The government of Israel "now assert[ed] its title to the territory over which its authority is actually exercised," and was concerned that, "in its endeavor to bridge the gap between the two parties, the Commission ha[d] placed on record certain conclusions which tend[ed] to prejudge the issue, thus defeating the purpose which the Commission [was] so earnestly pursuing." In particular, Eban objected to the PCC's assertion that Israel's proposals did "not form a practical basis upon which the work of conciliation could be usefully pursued," as well as the depiction of its territorial claims as "excessive."

> Such judgments on the merits of the issue by a body charged only with conciliation weight the scales against the party concerned and prejudice the whole outcome of the negotiations.

The commission's indication that it would be making specific suggestions was described by the Israeli representative as "an approach which call[ed] in[to] question the whole method of conciliation hitherto followed, and the terms of reference of the Commission itself."

Another key ingredient in Eban's letter to the PCC was his critique of the "stubborn refusal of the Arab States concerned to meet the Government of Israel around a conference table under the auspices of the Commission." Invoking the wording of UNGA resolution 194, he accused the Arabs of foiling the PCC's efforts at seeking agreement "by negotiation conducted either with the Conciliation commission or directly." It was, Eban argued, this "persistent refusal" which was responsible for the deadlock, and which had "led the commission to adopt methods which, in the conviction of the Government of Israel, [were] not conducive to success."

> While the Arab States maintain their negative attitude on the basic issue of peace with Israel, no conciliation is of any avail. Indeed, their very refusal to meet Israel in normal direct negotiations can only be interpreted as a lack of intention to reach a final settlement at this time. The continuation of the conciliation effort under these circumstances can only serve to becloud the real position, to vitiate the issue and to conceal the responsibility of the guilty party from world opinion.

Israel was therefore "driven by experience" to the conclusion that "the continuation of the conciliation effort under these circumstances" was "fruitless" and might well prove "harmful." This apparent Israeli abandonment of UN conciliation efforts was accompanied by a renewed initiative for direct contacts with individual Arab states, along with a softening of Washington's and London's attitude against separate bilateral negotiations.[9]

Lobbying the State Department

Even after clarifications were received from Jerusalem to the effect that Israel was not rejecting further negotiations with the commission, Eban's letter became "the principal matter of concern" to the PCC during a rare meeting with American officials at the State Department. While the meeting was devoted in part to preparing an "unequivocal reply... refuting the assertions made by Israel," Assistant Secretary McGhee shifted the discussion by encouraging the PCC to "make continued efforts to urge the parties to undertake direct talks," even though he appreciated the difficulties involved. The French and Turkish representatives assured their State Department hosts that they remained committed to attempting such meetings, but pointed to their inability to compel the Arab delegations to do so against their will. The commissioners also came away from the meeting with some

State Department encouragement for their proposal to move from "conciliation" to a more active form of "mediation."[10] A "reliable friend" of Israel who attended the meeting reported that the latest crisis in Israel-PCC relations had "increased anti-Israel feelings [in the] State Department, fortifying their complaints [that Israel was] deliberately obstructing UN authority, [and a] settlement."[11]

Several days later, Arab states began a concerted campaign for the US to pressure Israel to honor its "obligations" (as the Arabs interpreted them) under the Lausanne Protocol. The Iraqi government — which had abstained from both the armistice talks and the Lausanne conference — now took an active part in pressing the American government on this matter. An *aide-mémoire* handed to the US embassy in Baghdad denounced "the bad faith of the Jews" for failure to implement the Lausanne Protocol. This document was now presented as "some kind of gentleman's agreement" between the Arabs and the US in that (a) it bore the signatures of representatives of the Arab states and the US government, and (b) the Arabs had been led to believe by several earlier official statements of American policy indicating that the US would be prepared to implement a Palestine settlement which corresponded to Arab views of right and justice.[12] Despite its dissatisfaction and its reasons for remaining aloof in the past, the Iraqi government was now offering to "agree to what the Arab states bordering on Palestine have agreed" if the American government were to exercise its influence so as to "bring the Jews to honor their signature [to the Lausanne Protocol] and the obligations resulting from it."[13]

A week later, the ambassadors of seven Arab states were received by Acting Secretary Webb at the State Department where they submitted a joint memorandum. The Egyptian ambassador spoke for the group and explained that their visit was at the behest of a recent meeting of the Arab League Council. The ambassador referred to Israel's apparent refusal of "further collaboration with the Palestine Conciliation Commission" as the latest example of its lack of goodwill and cooperation. The memorandum — large parts of which were identical in wording to the Iraqi *aide-mémoire* — alluded to the recent Arab League meeting at which it was decided to form a common front for the purpose of "defending the peace against any danger from whatever source," and appealed to America's declared interest in "preserving peace in this particularly sensitive part of the world." The memorandum ended by expressing the Arab states' hope

> that the United States Government will not hesitate in giving them assurances that the peaceful solution concluded by common agreement at Lausanne in the protocol of May 12, 1949 will produce its full and complete effects, and that the United States Government will endeavor by using the effective means at its disposal and by direct action with the other interested party, to expedite this solution.[14]

The publicity following the Arab ambassadors' meeting at the State Department, especially the Arab criticism of Israel's uncooperative attitude, caused Israelis some concern.[15]

In his oral reply to the Arab diplomats, James Webb pointed to the UN and the PCC as more appropriate channels, and added some remarks about the desirability of Arabs and Israelis taking the initiative in advancing towards a settlement through direct talks. Both he and George McGhee reiterated the State Department position that the US "would not advance any specific solution to either party," leaving it to "the parties themselves [to] reach a mutually satisfactory agreement."[16] On the same day, during Anglo-American consultations in Washington, McGhee expressed the US view that, although "there was no quick solution" in sight, his government supported the continuation of the work of the PCC. In the face of some arguments currently being advanced for abolishing the three-man commission (representing three countries) and/or replacing it by a single mediator,[17] American policy remained committed to the PCC:

> Its affairs appeared at the moment to be in a critical state as a result of the Israelis' refusal to utilize it for indirect talks, and the Arabs' unwillingness to talk direct[ly] to the Jews. The United States delegate to the PCC would, however, urge the commission to seek a solution in every way possible, including encouragement of direct talks. If acceptable to both parties, the commission would mediate

between the disputants.[18]

Gradually, and in spite of Israeli reluctance, the PCC would move during 1950 and 1951 from "conciliation" to "mediation," culminating in September 1951 in US representative Ely Palmer staking out a new activist role for the commission, complete with a package of proposals to submit to the parties at a new peace conference in Paris.

CHAPTER 13

Conclusions

The work and the image of the PCC have often been compared unfavorably with those of the UN mediator, Count Bernadotte, and especially his successor, Ralph Bunche. Analyses of the PCC differ only in the strength of their language in bemoaning the commission's "heartbreaking efforts," its "exercise in futility" or its "unmitigated failure."[1] Recalling his own government's leadership role in the commission a year after Lausanne, Ambassador James G. McDonald in Tel Aviv deplored the fact that

> Ethridge, Porter and now Palmer [had] struggled valiantly and vainly against inherent organizational defects and inertia and bureaucracy of their colleagues which have made [the] PCC [a] mockery in [the] N[ear] E[ast].[2]

The comparison with Bernadotte and Bunche becomes even more striking if one accepts the view that "the circumstances that prevailed when the Conciliation Commission was launched were particularly propitious for a settlement" and that the UN and the powers missed a "golden opportunity" for Middle East peacemaking.[3]

While the reconstruction in the preceding pages does indeed reinforce some of the negative judgments made about the commission, the resulting explanations of this "missed opportunity" are more intricate and nuanced. In his excellent analysis of the work of the PCC, political scientist Saadia Touval demonstrates (even without the full benefits of archival material) how complex the reasons were for the failure of the commission to live up to expectations.[4] Drawing upon the detailed reconstruction in the preceding pages, we shall conclude by examining three sets of factors which have been offered to explain the failure of the 1949 Lausanne peace process: (1) the attitudes and positions of the parties, (2) the ineffectiveness of the PCC, and (3) the ineffectiveness of the US role.

Much of the existing analysis and commentary about the PCC and its Lausanne effort tends to overemphasize factors relating to the commission itself and the US role, while understating the heavy responsibility of the main protagonists for the failure of the PCC, in general, and the Lausanne conference, in particular. The following catalogue is an attempt to redress the balance among the various explanations which have been offered. While there are varying degrees of truth in all of them, it would be simplistic to single out any one or two explanations as the "true" cause of the failure of the Lausanne peace process.

The Attitudes and Positions of the Parties

Under this heading, the following reasons for the failure of the Lausanne conference may be advanced:

a. the basically irreconcilable positions of the parties, and the growing conviction of each side that time worked in its favor, making unnecessary any serious concessions for the sake of an agreement with the other side;
b. the Arab tactic of using the Lausanne conference to achieve the return of the refugees, in order to weaken or subvert Israel rather than make peace with it;
c. the Israeli tactic of stalling at Lausanne, in an effort to consolidate the military gains of 1948-49 without having to offer significant concessions on territory or a return of refugees.

Recent historical studies have begun to place appropriate emphasis on the attitudes, positions, motives and tactics of the parties themselves. Benny Morris, for example, has concluded that

> the basic incompatibility of the initial starting positions and the

> unwillingness of the two sides to move, and to move quickly, towards a compromise — born of Arab rejectionism and a deep feeling of humiliation, and of Israeli drunkenness with victory and physical needs determined by the Jewish refugee influx — doomed the "conference" from the start.[5]

But, even before delving into the motives and *bona fides* of either party, one must also take into account the impact of the aftermath of the 1948-49 fighting on the negotiations. The comparison with the success achieved at Rhodes takes on a more realistic light when one probes the intricate link between the military-strategic and political-bargaining situations. As one Israeli diplomat has argued,

> [t]he Arabs signed the armistice agreements [at Rhodes] because they had an urgent need to do so. The I[srael] D[efense] F[orce] was on the offensive on all fronts and only by means of armistice agreements could it be stopped.... At the time when the armistice agreements were signed the Arabs had no intention of making peace. They had a pressing interest in putting an end to the fighting and it was for this reason, and only this reason, that they signed the armistice agreements.[6]

Through accidents of timing, the Rhodes and Lausanne negotiating tracks proceeded separately in a way which resulted in "the political negotiations [being] insulated from military considerations." By the time the parties convened at Lausanne, three of the four armistice agreements were already signed. At this stage, Touval points out, "the parties no longer faced the risk of military confrontation. The pressure on them to make the concessions necessary for a settlement was thus greatly reduced."

> [N]either side enjoyed a decisive advantage, nor felt stalemated. Rather, both sides considered their position as bearable.... [S]ince both sides expected that if they stood fast the situation might improve, the circumstances were not propitious for successful mediation.[7]

The commission itself noted, retrospectively in late 1950, these very reasons for failure: once the armistice agreements, which included "undertakings of non-aggression of unlimited validity," had been signed, this had "the effect of eliminating military considerations and of greatly reducing, in the minds of the parties, the immediate necessity of taking further steps towards a final settlement."[8] Seen from an Israeli perspective at the time, all the PCC and American pressure on Israel for gestures on refugee repatriation or territorial adjustments proved to be a further obstacle to peace, because these pressures offset or canceled out the results of the military confrontation which had recently ended:

> the Arabs, seeing that very important and influential elements took their side, saw no need to comply with a settlement based on the reality created after the fighting and the armistice agreements.[9]

Whatever the failings of the PCC and its American backers, the commission was faced at every turn with near-insurmountable obstacles posed by the hardening positions of the parties themselves. Beneath all the public platitudes about desiring peace and wishing to cooperate with the UN peace effort, the diplomatic activity of Arabs and Israelis at Lausanne could be characterized as posturing and maneuvering so as to avoid accepting solutions which fell short of their respective goals. In Israel's case, the objective was to consolidate the *status quo* and, in the case of the Arab states, it was to revert as much as possible to the *status quo ante.*

Several of the Lausanne participants have written bitterly about the selfishness, stubbornness and/or unreasonableness of one or more of the main protagonists. These very personal and partisan testimonies are uncompromising in their condemnation of the designated guilty party — whether it is Eytan, Sasson or Azcárate denouncing the Arab states' cynical exploitation of the refugee issue, or Shuqayri condemning Israeli insensitivity and intransigence. One participant who was able to experience the worst of both camps was Muhammad Nimr al-Hawwari, who represented one group of Palestinian refugees. In his view, both the Arab and Israeli delegations behaved as though time was on their side.

> The Arabs stalled and procrastinated, believing that keeping Israel

> under threat would lead to its economic collapse, since it would be forced to keep its army in a constant state of alert. The Israelis wanted to use the pressing problem of the refugees in order to prod the Arab states into making peace with it.

But, as for the refugees,

> they were like the prey over which wild beasts were fighting. Time was working against the refugees. Neither the Arab states nor Israel would be harmed by the passage of time, for, unlike the situation of the refugees, none of their residents would starve or be stranded in the wilderness.[10]

Even Eliahu Sasson, the Israeli delegate entrusted with the task of maintaining informal contacts with Hawwari and other Arabs at Lausanne, delivered a blistering critique, just before the recess, of all the participants — including the lack of coherence and realism of his own country's negotiating aims and tactics.[11]

Part of Israel's apparent stalling at Lausanne was due to greater energies and hopes being diverted to its preferred avenue of direct, bilateral talks with each Arab state separately. When the PCC's chosen format at Lausanne showed no signs of providing for such negotiating opportunities, Israelis reactivated their direct links with Abdallah and his confidants. The operation of this separate track of secret Israel-Jordan talks naturally led both the Israeli and Jordanian delegates at Lausanne to devote less serious attention to the plodding, multilateral conference. The Jerusalem question, in particular, saw Israel's interests coinciding with Abdallah's in rejecting internationalization, and this "provided a powerful incentive for bypassing the PCC and seeking to reach a bilateral accord."[12] Yet, the evidence examined in the preceding pages would not seem to warrant historian Ilan Pappé's claim that the Lausanne conference "opened the way to all kinds of possibilities," but that Israel's preference for bilateral talks with Jordan resulted in missed opportunities which were "not properly explored, let alone tested."[13]

Although we have not attempted in these pages to assess what might have happened if certain opportunities had not been missed by one or another of the parties, such assessments have been advanced in other writings. Pappé, for example, has recently speculated that the outcome of the Lausanne conference might have been different if the Israeli delegation had taken a less negative approach to the protocol of 12 May, and had sought to create a more positive "momentum and orientation in the peace process" — especially in the light of the gradual growth of Arab enthusiasm for the protocol.[14] It is difficult to imagine successful negotiations emerging from a situation in which the Arab side interpreted Israel's signature on the protocol as indicating acceptance of the 1947 partition plan as a basis of discussion. Furthermore, Pappé does not consider the possibility that this Arab enthusiasm for the protocol was in many ways a *product* of Israel's negative reaction.

Likewise, Rony Gabbay's pioneering and meticulously detailed 1959 study of the refugee problem suggested that "[h]ad Israel, in March-May 1949, accepted the right of the refugees to return to their homes and lands, the history of the region during the last ten years might have taken a different course."[15] Indeed, unknown to Gabbay and other early scholars, Walter Eytan had toyed with that very idea during the conference. With the aim of relieving the pressure on his delegation in mid-June, Eytan wondered whether Israel might find a harmless formula for accepting UNGA resolution 194's call for the repatriation of refugees, in "a careful letter, not giving away anything vital on our side, but granting the bare principle upon which, say the Arabs and Palestine Conciliation Commission, everything depends."[16] In the end, the negative Israeli negotiating strategy was not altered regarding either repatriation or the protocol. It seems highly speculative and far from convincing to argue that such changes would have led to any breakthrough or significant softening of the Arab position.[17] It would appear to be equally unproductive to ask (as no scholars have yet done) whether a change in the *Arab position* — e.g., agreement to face-to-face meetings, Egypt's consent to discuss the Gaza proposal — would have led to Israeli compromises and a possible breakthrough to a peace accord. Instead of speculating on the "what-ifs" of history, a thorough and sober look at the positions and strategies which the parties felt compelled to adopt reveals how and why a deadlock was produced and maintained, and how no carrots or sticks brandished by outsiders proved capable of altering that fact. Just as the Israelis were determined to ensure that Lausanne did not produce any significant reduction of their territorial acquisitions or large-scale repatriation of refugees, so too were the Arab delegations bent on using the Lausanne peace process to force Israel to accept the 1947 partition boundaries and a return of the Palestinian refugees before they would consider any thought of concluding peace arrangements.

The Ineffectiveness of the PCC

Under this heading, four explanations for the failure of the Lausanne conference have been advanced, and we shall examine each of them in turn.

a. *The PCC suffered from the weaknesses inherent in a three-member body, as opposed to a single conciliator/mediator. This weakness was also evident in the vulnerability of the Commission to interference from the home governments of the three appointing powers.*

One positive interpretation of the PCC's composition was that the three powers, acting in concert, could have wielded a combined influence over the various Middle Eastern states that would have greatly enhanced the effectiveness of the PCC.[18] Against this was the negative view of the PCC as a "three-headed monster."[19] Ben-Gurion, for example, explained his lack of faith in the outcome of the Lausanne conference partly because, unlike the single-minded peace-seeker Ralph Bunche, members of the commission were influenced by "other aspirations" dictated by their governments.[20] Ahmad Shuqayri felt the initial members of the commission formed "an incongruous formation... which was in need of a conciliation commission to be created among its varying and separate personalities."[21] Indeed, although the PCC was officially mandated and paid by the UN, to which it submitted periodic reports, each of the three representatives on the PCC was heavily dependent on his home government for advice and practical support. Despite the international task at hand, the commissioners regularly sought guidance from Washington, Paris and Istanbul, whose interests and policies became inextricably bound up in the work of the commission.

But did the various "national interests" of the powers "frequently [take] precedence over the requirements of conciliation," as some have suggested?[22] It is difficult to find any hard evidence of the PCC's quest for peace being diverted because of subservience to any selfish national interests of one of the appointing powers. Neither does the reconstruction offered in the preceding pages reveal any major breakdown of the PCC's operations due to serious differences among the three members or their home governments. Only in August, when Paul Porter sought (in defiance of Secretary Acheson's caution) to work out a tentative consensus on territorial proposals did the interests of France, Turkey and the US pull in different directions.[23] The exercise merely confirmed the State Department's reluctance to see the PCC attempt a mediatory role with its own set of peace proposals.

Because the three heads of the so-called monster were not equal, one cannot rightly ascribe to its composition the flaw of indecision. Within the PCC, there was no doubt as to which of the three members was the dominant partner. In the words of one of the Israeli negotiators at Lausanne, both France and Turkey were "hitched to the American wagon." Mark Ethridge, another Israeli delegate commented, was "clearly out to conquer the Middle East for America, and Boisanger and Yalchin appear[ed] to be not unwilling to help him."[24] Touval goes so far as to suggest that "the commission became an instrument of US diplomacy" — a view entertained by most Israeli officials involved in the Lausanne peace process.[25] While these comments tend to overstate the case, they do contradict the notion that being a three-member body resulted in a lack of direction on the part of the PCC. In one of their subsequent annual reviews of the failures and future of the PCC, the US State Department and the British Foreign

Office found themselves in agreement that "the reasons for the PCC's failure [were] inherent in the situation rather than in the machinery for dealing with it."[26]

b. *The Commission failed to mobilize effective support from the home governments of the three appointing powers.*

This view of the PCC maintains that it acted "with inexplicable timidity" at Lausanne, given the potential "tremendous" prestige which it enjoyed, having among its members the US and France, both holding permanent seats on the UN Security Council. The commission had at its disposal, this critique continues, "plenty of leverage" which it "chose" not to use and the potential of its prestige was not "properly committed."[27]

Although this criticism has been made from an Israeli perspective, our reconstruction from the archival documents shows that its most forceful proponents at the time were Arabs. Seen from an Arab perspective, the timidity of the PCC manifested itself in a lack of determination to ensure compliance with UN resolutions, thus leaving Israel, *de facto*, enjoying the fruits of its defiance of world opinion.

As we have seen, the Arab states were among the most enthusiastic supporters of the idea of a stronger mediation role for the PCC and the United Nations, often pressing for an imposed solution. Such a solution would have been based, they hoped, on forcing Israel to concede territories gained during the war (*via* the November 1947 partition resolution) and to accept the return of Palestinian refugees (*via* the December 1948 resolution). Indeed, this demand for PCC mediation (rather than conciliation), coupled with the Arab states' refusal to meet directly with the Israelis, formed the essence of the Arab tactical position of the period. The Arabs believed their approach

> would ultimately drive the commission into a position where it would have to make proposals of its own. The calculations were no doubt to put the three countries represented on the commission 'on the spot' as regards their policies toward Israel and the Arab states in the Middle East; they very likely felt that regardless of what the

> Commission might propose, it would not be in favor of the Israel position, and so far as the Arabs were concerned, it would be that much gained for them and would serve as a base from which they could carry on further bargaining.[28]

Before, during, and immediately after Lausanne, the PCC disappointed the Arabs by not assuming this sort of interventionist role. But it was not as weak, inept or unaware of its potential as has sometimes been suggested. The criticism that the commissioners were naively "convinced that the prestige of their sponsor, the UN, sufficed to guarantee the success of their endeavors"[29] does not appear well-founded. As Dr. Bunche had done during his pursuit of the armistice talks, the PCC appealed regularly to Washington to apply leverage to help coax one or more of the parties to adopt more flexible positions. But, as the American secretary of state felt forced to admit in mid-October 1949, all US efforts to persuade Arabs and Israelis to be more reasonable towards the PCC's peace effort had simply "had no appreciable effect on [the] position of either party."[30]

c. *The personalities and talents of the men chosen to sit on the Commission were unsuited and unequal to their task.*

Both the PCC's principal secretary and the American ambassador in Tel Aviv attributed a fair share of the failure of the PCC's efforts to individual personality factors of the various commissioners.[31] This impression also emerges from Arab and Israeli participants at Lausanne. Ahmad Shuqayri had difficulty taking seriously what he called "that collection of retired diplomats" and "left-overs" from bygone eras.[32] Israelis found reason to draw unfavorable comparisons between Ralph Bunche's "persistent optimism [about] success" and Mark Ethridge's "morbid fear of failure."[33] Both Ethridge and his successor, Paul Porter, displayed an "impetuosity" and an impatience for results which often conflicted with Claude de Boisanger's slower pace.[34] For his part, de Boisanger was (mistakenly) under the impression that the Americans wished to give the PCC broader authority so as to use it as a channel for implementing US Middle East policy.[35] Shuqayri mocked the elderly Turkish member's tendency to be "noiseless," while Ethridge considered him "rather past his prime."[36] Hussein Yalçin, for his part, held his own unflattering views of the motives and abilities of his French and American colleagues.[37]

While the operations of the PCC were no doubt less effective as a result of these personality factors and the parties' reservations about the PCC's composition and functioning, this element accounts for only part of an overall explanation for the commission's failure.

d. *The inexperienced commissioners committed several tactical errors, especially their unwillingness or inability to get the Arabs to agree to direct meetings with the Israelis.*

In his memoirs, Muhammad Nimr al-Hawwari blamed the frustration and deadlock at Lausanne on the fact that all negotiation was "centered on formalities and superficial issues," thanks to the PCC's less-than-skillful execution of its intermediary role.[38] Touval points to a number of serious tactical errors for which he holds the commission responsible. In particular, he suggests that the results at Lausanne might have been more successful had the PCC (a) become directly involved in the armistice negotiations from the start, thereby linking (rather than separating) the military from the political talks; and (b) not projected the Palestinian refugee issue at such an early stage "onto center stage," thereby

> encourag[ing] the Arabs to take a rigid position [and] strengthen[ing] the Israeli impression that the commission's approach and conception of its task were detrimental to Israeli interests.[39]

As we have seen, Sharett, Sasson and most Israeli officials during 1949 considered the most distressing feature of the PCC's method of operation to be its failure to force the Arab delegations to negotiate directly with Israel in accordance with the "Rhodes model" — i.e., (a) separately (as opposed to collectively), and (b) directly (as opposed to indirectly, *via* the commission). Even after Lausanne, the UNTSO chief, General William Riley, and the experienced British minister in Amman, Sir Alec Kirkbride, continued to attribute the PCC's failure primarily to its initial agreement to meet the Arabs jointly in Beirut, and its "refusal" to deal with the Arab states individually at Lausanne.[40] Even Ralph Bunche believed that the PCC "had... destroyed all chances of its own success when it decided at Beirut to negotiate with the Arab States as a bloc rather than individually."[41]

A number of scholarly analyses have echoed this criticism in varying degrees. Mordechai Gazit, a retired diplomat and scholar of mediation, has written that "[i]t is not clear why [the PCC] did not emulate Dr. Bunche's successful technique of organizing face-to-face meetings under UN auspices."[42] Avi Shlaim considers "the procedure adopted by the PCC and its effect of welding the Arabs into one party" as "a contributory cause" of the failure of the Lausanne conference. David Forsythe, in his pioneering study of the PCC, refers to "the decision to treat the Arab states *en bloc*" as a "tactical error."[43] Nadav Safran goes further and echoes the views of Eytan and Sasson in calling it a "fatal mistake."[44] A more extreme corollary to this criticism is that, beginning with its convening of the Beirut conference of March 1949, the PCC actually *created* an Arab "bloc" which proved detrimental to successful negotiations.[45]

Pablo de Azcárate, who is severely critical of the commission on other matters, finds this "oft-repeated accusation... as gratuitous as it is unjustified," while a member of the Israeli Lausanne delegation claims, in retrospect, that "the explanation that the conference failed because the Arab representatives appeared together rather than separately is childish."[46] In its *Eighth Progress Report* (October 1950), the PCC looked back to its beginnings and downplayed the importance of the Beirut meetings as forming an important precedent, and noted also that at Lausanne the Arab delegations had "insisted" on being treated "as a single block."[47]

The evidence which we have seen suggests that, rather than second-guessing the PCC for tactical errors in this regard, one should examine the existing political maneuvering among the Arab states, which was clearly moving towards the creation of a common front in any case, i.e., coordination of their policies and interests on the

Palestine issue. Beginning in early 1949, most of the diplomatic activity among the Arabs was dedicated to emphasizing the return of the refugees under resolution 194 while avoiding separate peace arrangements with Israel in a repetition of the Rhodes format. It was impossible for the commissioners not to notice this trend; neither were they able to sidestep this reality. At Beirut, the conference was, in the words of the PCC secretary, "the only thing the commission could do to avert the danger of finding itself paralyzed before having advanced a single step along the road the Assembly had marked out for it."[48]

While advancing some possible logistical justifications for the PCC's preference for collective rather than separate dealings with the Arab states, Saadia Touval is more critical of the PCC for "not insisting that the Arabs and Israelis negotiate face to face — even though direct negotiations are no guarantee of success." In his view, the commission's acceptance of the Arab refusal to meet Israeli representatives

> implicitly condoned Arab intransigence, and encouraged the Arab states to maintain rigid negotiating positions. Acceptance of the Arab view on this point undermined the Conciliation Commission's standing and effectiveness from the Israeli viewpoint.[49]

As convincing as Touval's analysis is, it is equally conceivable that, the PCC — having obtained Arab acceptance of the Lausanne invitation on the condition there would be no direct talks with Israelis — was faced with a choice between indirect conciliation or no Arab participation at all.[50] We are left with the conclusion that Mordechai Gazit is perhaps correct when he states that "[t]he question whether progress would have been possible in Lausanne had the commission operated differently belongs to the unanswered 'ifs' of history."[51]

The US Role

Under this heading we shall examine three explanations which have been advanced for the failure of the Lausanne conference.

a. *The US lacked a clear policy regarding a solution.*

More than fifteen years after Lausanne, PCC Secretary Pablo de Azcárate reflected bitterly about "the inconstancy and volatility of the American government's policy (if it can be called policy to have none)."[52] In a more temperate vein, one scholar of the PCC has criticized American policy at the close of the Lausanne efforts as being "something less than clear."[53]

On the weight of the evidence examined above, it is difficult to accept such criticisms at their face value. As Barry Rubin has aptly observed, calling for "a clear and consistent US foreign policy" on any given issue has become "one of the hoariest *clichés* in American politics."

> It is no accident that this goal is virtually never attained. A myriad of interests and countries, rapidly changing situations, necessarily conflicting relationships, and the need to bargain or bluff with other states require a certain lack of clarity and a measure of apparent inconsistency.[54]

In fact, having helped to establish and guide the commission before and during Lausanne, the American position on the future of PCC efforts in the fall of 1949 was clearer than ever. At an important American diplomatic policy conference in Istanbul (26-29 November), it was decided that the US should continue support for the commission, but should also "encourage direct negotiations between Israel and the Arab States" without

> abandon[ing] publicly its principles on refugees and territories. It should refrain from suggesting the nature of any settlement, leaving this to be determined by the relative bargaining positions of the parties.[55]

Secretary Acheson's written reply to the Arab diplomats'

memorandum of late 1949 reflected this outlook, and spelled out the US position authoritatively and clearly:

> One of the principal objectives of the United States with respect to the Palestine problem is the restoration of peace and stability in the Near Eastern area. The United States Government is convinced that it is in the best interest of the parties themselves that they should take the initiative in advancing from the armistice stage to that of permanent peace and that they should employ all means at their disposal, including direct negotiations, to achieve this end.
>
> The United States Government stands ready to assist the Arab States and Israel, both as a member of the Palestine Conciliation Commission and in such other ways as may seem desirable, in achieving a final settlement of the Palestine question.[56]

The same basic message regarding the American approach was passed informally to the Israelis by the American ambassador in Tel Aviv, while guidelines summarizing the outcome of the Istanbul Conference for US chiefs of mission stated:

> the United States, while maintaining strict impartiality and continuing to support the PCC and the ESM as means of solving outstanding issues, favors direct negotiations as offering the best possibility of obtaining agreement between the parties concerned.[57]

b. *The US did not provide sufficient US backing for the efforts of the PCC.*

In his memoirs, Azcárate complained that the absence of a clear American policy "left the Commission without the moral and political support which was the indispensable condition for its very existence and functioning."[58] Touval's analysis clearly refutes the argument (advanced also by Forsythe and Khouri) that the PCC failed because of a lack of US backing.[59] As indicated elsewhere, the unofficial role played by the United States at Lausanne cannot be underestimated. Without this American involvement, the commission would have exerted even less influence than it managed to exert on the parties. For Arabs as for Israelis in 1949, winning the favor and avoiding the displeasure of a world power like America meant very real benefits or drawbacks: economic aid, lifting of the arms embargo (in force between May 1948 and August 1949), future military aid, recognition, etc. These considerations provided a realistic motivation for the parties to consider, on occasion, making a concession to the other side. While Americans brandished both carrots and sticks before the recalcitrant Israelis, they had but few carrots and no sticks with which to win Arab cooperation.[60]

It seems fair to conclude, as one Israeli scholar has done, that the limited achievements of the Lausanne conference were due, in large measure, to "American pressure on the victorious party in the war, an on the whole obstinate Israel, to concede to some of the demands of the defeated, but on the whole unrealistic Arab countries."[61] American hesitation about supporting Israel's admission to the United Nations did, as we have seen, contribute to that country's reluctant signature of the Lausanne Protocol. Benny Morris cites the family reunion program as another "minor fruit" of US involvement, and credits Sharett's appreciation of American pressure as one of the incentives for making the offer to repatriate 100,000 refugees. True, these Israeli offers fell short of what the US government hoped to obtain; but "even these concessions would not have been offered without American pressure."[62] Although they were not attractive enough to lead to a settlement with the Arabs, these half-hearted concessions were sufficient, in the end, to "help Israel sail through the Lausanne Conference without a lasting crisis in its relations with the United States."[63]

What was the true extent and impact of US intervention? Drawing on the conclusions of Nadav Safran and Fred J. Khouri, Saadia Touval discerns two conflicting criticisms of the US role:

> i) by exerting *too much* interference, the US upset Israel's relative postwar military advantage and shielded the Arab states from having to negotiate under pressure, thereby producing a stalemate where there might have been an agreement (close to Israel's terms);[64] and ii) by *not enough* intervention, the US allowed Israel to maintain its upper hand over the defeated Arabs, thereby failing to create the balance (or 'stalemate') necessary for successful negotiations.[65]

The weight of the evidence assembled in the current study would suggest that the State Department was consciously attempting to steer a middle course in an unsuccessful attempt to avoid either unhelpful result. However, in the course of this effort, and as the deadlock persisted, the US managed to create perceptions of *both* too much interference (in Israeli eyes) *and* not enough intervention (in Arab eyes).

As we have seen, the Americans did not, in spite of early intentions to do so, play a strong interventionist role in terms of proposing their own ideas for a solution. This was the State Department's consistent line during 1949, despite (a) pressure to do so coming from both British and Arab quarters and even from some of its own advisers, and (b) the existence, on the public record, of both the Jessup principle (defining American suggestions for a territorial settlement) and very specific State Department ideas about refugee repatriation and resettlement. In spite of all this, by mid-October a National Security Council report still spoke of the American position as preferring to see "a solution freely agreed to by the parties."[66]

Yet, even though it refused to promote specific terms of a settlement, it would be incorrect to accuse the State Department of adopting a stand-aside or *laissez-faire* attitude. Pressure on the Israelis for a gesture was persistent and occasionally strong. Even if it yielded few dramatic results, such pressure "slowly wore down Israeli obduracy."[67] But there were also times when American pressure may have been so heavy-handed as to have been counterproductive. As Forsythe has suggested with regard to the Truman note of rebuke of 29 May:

> Far from achieving its intended objective, this abruptly applied and hastily withdrawn attempt at exerting influence had antagonized Israel, impaired future US power, and had had the indirect effect of weakening the [PCC] since it discredited the commission's most powerful member.[68]

The American offer of good offices to Egypt in pursuit of negotiations on the Gaza proposal is another example illustrating the limitations of American influence. The failure of the initiative may well have been due to the fact that the original Israeli proposal was a nonstarter from so many points of view. But the fact remains that Dean Acheson, on the best advice of his officials, pursued it forcefully in the hope that it would prove to be the key to a breakthrough. Through its less-than-skillful promotion of the Gaza proposal, the US ventured — and lost — important political credibility in London, Cairo and Tel Aviv.

If the above may appear to be sins of commission, some have suggested that there may have been a missed opportunity for a breakthrough in early August, when the US and the commission failed to provide a more concerted effort either "to persuade the Arab governments to accept Israel's offer or to make a counteroffer that would bridge the gap between [the Arab demand for] total repatriation and the limited [Israeli] offer of 100,000."[69] But current research seems to indicate that there was no "missed opportunity" here. A recent scholarly investigation of Israeli documents has convincingly shown "that the offer was made without any intention of implementation and that it would not have been made had there been any realistic prospect of its acceptance by the Arabs."[70]

The late appearance of the 100,000 offer must also be taken into account: Morris has called it a classic example of "too little, too late."[71] The offer appeared on the scene after months of representations, arguments, pressures and counter-arguments in pursuit of an Israeli gesture and in attempts to start talks on the Gaza proposal. By this point, all parties were justifiably weary and cynical. Israel seemed determined not to budge from the 100,000 figure, and the other parties had little optimism or energy to invest in trying to build a negotiating opportunity around this latest unattractive proposal.

c. *The US was unwilling or unable to apply necessary pressure on Israel for concessions that would have unblocked various impasses.*

Benny Morris has noted that American pressures on both sides were inadequate because they lacked "a sharp, determined cutting edge."[72] Others have argued that a power like the US might have leaned more heavily — or, at least, more effectively and consistently — than it did on a dependent young state like Israel. But the evidence assembled in the current study does not validate the simplistic claim that "[t]he United States did not... try to exert any pressure on Israel."[73] We have seen that the US State Department attempted to utilize all its available carrots and sticks with the Israelis. The fact that all the coaxing, representations and rebukes brought few results at Lausanne is no indictment of the State Department for lack of concern or effort.

Likewise, it would be misleading to argue that the US involvement in the Lausanne peace process was unhelpful because it was heavily tilted in favor of the Israelis. Historian Itamar Rabinovich and others have rightly pointed out that, during the Lausanne effort, the US position — based as it was on UNGA resolution 194 and the Jessup principle — was both publicly and privately supportive of many *Arab*, not Israeli, demands on the main issues of the day: Jerusalem, refugees and territory. "Consequently, the American effort to advance the PCC's work was manifested primarily in pressure exerted on Israel."[74]

A more convincing case could be made that this pro-Arab tilt of the US contributed to the failure of Lausanne — precisely, as Touval has argued, because the Arabs knew that the American position on the major issues was so close to their own. It was this awareness that led the Arab states to the false hope that the United States would be able to deliver a change in Israel's stance:

> The result was that American policy actually served to encourage the Arabs to stand fast and not compromise.... [T]he Arab states were led to expect that the United States would make Israel admit a substantial portion of the refugees, and give up the Negev and perhaps other areas it held. This expectation prevented the Arab governments from softening their stand and accepting less than the US told them that it would obtain for them.[75]

Our detailed look at the record reveals a number of clear indications that the Arab delegations at Lausanne were definitely encouraged to believe that they could count on both American and British support for their position on territorial compromise and refugee repatriation.[76]

But when it came to questions regarding the negotiating process—

i.e., the clear discouragement of appeals for greater US involvement in PCC mediation, the encouragement of direct talks between the parties — the State Department gradually aligned itself far more closely with the *Israeli* than the Arab position. The impact upon the main protagonists was to add to the Arabs' disappointment while encouraging the Israelis.

The foregoing lends credence to Touval's suggestion that the ineffectiveness of the American role was due neither to lack of effort, nor to partiality towards either party; rather, he argues, it was the inconsistency in US expectations of, and signals to, the adversaries that led to a hardening, rather than the intended softening, of their respective bargaining positions.[77] During 1948-1949, the United States seems to have inherited from the British the role of appearing, to some, as an all-powerful arbiter. But this external perception was not matched by the reality on the ground. The former British masters of Palestine also bequeathed to the Americans the unenviable and near-impossible chore of maintaining the trust of Israelis and Arabs simultaneously.

Rhodes had been a success in terms of its limited goals of converting a cease-fire into an armistice. Getting the parties to come to the table, albeit separate tables, at Lausanne to discuss more complex political issues required much cajoling. However, getting them to negotiate a comprehensive settlement there proved an impossible task. America's "*presumed* ability, as a great power, to exert the influence necessary to make the adversaries change their policies"[78] was just not operative. Against those who imagined that the PCC was but a sinister front for an interventionist American policy, we have seen evidence of senior policymakers like George McGhee declaring that

> it was the United States, policy to keep the solution of the Palestine question in a United Nations framework and not to intervene on a national basis. The United States Government had decided that it was neither desirable nor possible for the United States itself to propose any overall solution. It was not considered that the United States had sufficient influence on the countries concerned to persuade them to accept such a solution, and the result would only be to create bad

> relations and impair the position of the United States in assisting the United Nations or the states concerned in arriving at an agreement.[79]

The Lausanne episode was one of a number of opportunities where the United States was forced to learn (and relearn) the real limitations of its ability to promote a solution to the intractable Arab-Israeli conflict.

NOTES

Introduction

1. For an excellent overview of Israel-Syria, Israel-Jordan and Israel-Egypt contacts between 1949 and 1952, see: Itamar Rabinovich, *The Road Not Taken: Early Arab-Israeli Negotiations,* New York/Oxford: Oxford University Press, 1991.
2. For an overview of UN peace-keeping and peacemaking, see Fred J. Khouri, "United Nations Peace Efforts," in *The Elusive Peace in the Middle East,* Malcolm H. Kerr (ed.) (Albany: State University of New York Press, 1975), 19-101.
3. Ilan Pappé, *The Making of the Arab-Israeli Conflict, 1947-51,* (London/New York: I.B. Tauris, 1992), 201.
4. Lovett to Ethridge, 19 Jan. 1949, reproduced in Saadia Touval, *The Peace Brokers: Mediators in the Arab-Israeli Conflict, 1948-1979,* (Princeton: Princeton University Press, 1982), 95-97.
5. For the text of the resolution, see: George J. Tomeh (ed.), *United Nations Resolutions on Palestine and the Arab-Israeli Conflict, vol. I:* 1947-1974, (Washington: Institute for Palestine Studies, 1975), 130. Cf. Touval, *Peace Brokers,* 60.
6. For the text of the resolution, see Tomeh, *United Nations Resolutions,* I:15-17. On the origins of the resolution, see Pappé, *Making,* 195f.; Avi Shlaim, *Collusion Across the Jordan: King Abdullah, the Zionist Movement, and the Partition of Palestine,* (Oxford: Clarendon Press, 1988), 461.
7. For an excellent attempt to learn from the past, see Kenneth W. Stein and Samuel W. Lewis (with Sheryl J. Brown), *Making Peace among Arabs and Israelis: Lessons from Fifty Years of Negotiating Experience,* Washington: United States Institute of Peace, October 1991.
8. See, e.g., Mordechai Gazit, "Mediation and Mediators," *Jerusalem Journal of International Relations,* 5:4 (1981), 80-83; Stein and Lewis, *Making Peace,* ix, 2.

Chapter 1

1. At Rhodes, Walter Eytan resented being pressed by an impatient PCC to finish up quickly. W. Eytan, "Eight Years After Rhodes," *Jerusalem Post,* 24 Feb. 1957.
2. Ethridge to Acheson, 8 Feb. 1949, United States, Department of State, *Foreign Relations of the United States: Diplomatic Papers: 1949,* vol.VI, (Washington: 1977), 735-38 (hereinafter: *FRUS 1949* VI); same to same, 8 Feb. 1949, quoted in ibid., 738 n.2; Shertok to Eban, 9 Feb. 1949, Israel State Archives, *Documents on the Foreign Policy of Israel,* vol.2 (October 1948 — April 1949), ed. Yehoshua Freundlich, (Jerusalem: 1984), 422-24 [D379], hereinafter: *ID2.* Cf. Memorandum on the Refugee Problem, 16 March 1949, *ID2,* 502-10 [D443].
3. Ethridge to Acheson, 8 Feb. 1949, discussed in *FRUS 1949* VI, 738 n.2; same to same, 28 Feb. 1949, ibid., 778 (which referred to Shertok's "rantings" during this meeting); James G. McDonald, *My Mission in Israel, 1948-1951,* (New York: Simon & Schuster, 1951), 177; Benny Morris, *The Birth of the Palestinian Refugee Problem, 1947-1949,* (Cambridge/New York: Cambridge University Press, 1987), 257.
4. Keeley-Azm conversation (8 Feb.), reported in Keeley to Acheson, 9 Feb. 1949 (tgm.50), USNA 501.BB Pal/2-949. Cf. *FRUS 1949* VI, 742 n.1.
5. Dorsz to Acheson, 20 Feb. 1949, *FRUS 1949* VI, 757f.
6. Ethridge to Acheson, 12 Feb. 1949, *FRUS 1949* VI, 744-46. Cf. Dayan to Dori and Shertok, 12 Feb. 1949, Israel State Archives, *Documents on the Foreign Policy of Israel,* vol. 3: Armistice Negotiations with the Arab States: December 1948-July 1949, ed. Yemima Rosenthal, (Jerusalem: 1983), 349 [D189], hereinafter: *ID3*; Pablo de Azcárate, *Mission in Palestine, 1948-1952,* (Washington: Middle East Institute, 1966), 143f.; Touval, *Peace Brokers,* 81, 93; Shlaim, *Collusion,* 468.
7. Patterson to Acheson, 14 Feb. 1949 (tgm.166), USNA 501.BB Pal/2-1449; cf. *FRUS 1949* VI, 750 n.1.
8. Ethridge to Acheson, 15 Feb. 1949, *FRUS 1949* VI, 750-52.
9. Ethridge to Acheson, 15 Feb. 1949, discussed in *FRUS 1949* VI, 752 n.4. The British ambassador echoed these views about the Egyptian-Israeli Rhodes talks. See Campbell to FO, 17 Feb. 1949 (tgm.272), in PRO FO371/75347 E2293/1017/31.
10. Two telegrams from Campbell to FO, 16 Feb. (tgm.36 Saving), and 17 Feb. 1949 (tgm.272), in PRO FO371/75347 E2291 and E2293/1017/31. For another report of the PCC visit to Cairo, see *al-Ahram,* 14 Feb. 1949, p.4.

11. Mack to FO, 21 Feb. 1949 (tgm.164), PRO FO371/75347 E2416/1017/31. For American and British reports of the PCC's tour, see: *FRUS 1949* VI, 756-58, 766f.; Dow to FO, 22 Feb. 1949 (tgm. 141), FO371/75347 E2429/1017/31. Cf. *al-Ahram*, 20 Feb. 1949 (dateline Baghdad, 19 Feb.), p.4; Azcárate, *Mission*, 144-47.
12. Acheson to Ethridge (Jerusalem), 25 Feb. 1949 (tgm.111), quoted in *FRUS 1949* VI, 772 n.1. Several days later, Ethridge replied that he was in essential agreement with this principle. Ibid., 780.
13. Ethridge's report of the meeting of 24 Feb. 1949, *FRUS 1949* VI, 772-74; the Israeli record of the meeting is *ID2*, 441-54 [D400]. Quotations in this and the following paragraphs are from these sources.
14. See, e.g., *ID4*, 495f., 578-82; *FRUS 1951* V, 935-40; *ID6* [1951], 808-19 and 836-39; Walter Eytan, *The First Ten Years: A Diplomatic History of Israel*, (New York: Simon & Schuster, 1958), 63f.; Shlaim, *Collusion*, 511f.; Shlomo Perla, "Israel and the Palestine Conciliation Commission," *Middle Eastern Studies* 26:1 (Jan. 1990), 113-18.
15. The Israeli government's decision, in principle, not to allow a return of the refugees had been taken during the summer of 1948. See: Benny Morris, "The Crystallization of Israeli Policy Against a Return of the Arab Refugees: April-December, 1948," *Studies in Zionism* 6:1 (Spring 1985), 85-118; Morris, *Birth*, 254f.
16. Meeting of 25 Feb., reported in (a) Ethridge to Acheson, 28 Feb. 1949, *FRUS 1949* VI, 775f. and (b) David Ben-Gurion, *Yoman ha-Milhama: Milhemet ha-Atzma'ut* (War Diary: The War of Independence, 1947-1949), ed. Gershon Rivlin and Elhanan Orren, (Tel Aviv: Ministry of Defense Publishing, 1982), 971.

Chapter 2

1. Ethridge to Acheson, 2 tgms. dated 28 Feb. 1949, *FRUS 1949* VI, 776-80. Cf. Morris, *Birth*, 257f.; Azcárate, *Mission*, 147f.
2. Shertok, in meeting with PCC, 24 Feb. 1949, *ID2*, 453 [D400]. Cf. Shiloah-McDonald talk (28 Feb.), reported in McDonald to Acheson, 1 March 1949, *FRUS 1949* VI, 785 n.1; David P. Forsythe, *United Nations Peacemaking: The Conciliation Commission for Palestine*, (Baltimore/London: Johns Hopkins University Press, 1972), 42f.
3. Mack to FO, 21 Feb. 1949 (tgm.164), PRO FO371/75347 E2416/1017/31; McDonald, *My Mission*, 178; Touval, *Peace Brokers*, 93; Pappé, *Making*, 201.
4. Sasson to Lourie, 12 March 1949, *ID2*, 495-97 [D435]. Cf. Elath to Sasson, 15 March 1949, ISA 130.20/2477/21/a; Eban-Chauvel conversation,

reported in Eban to Eytan, 2 April 1949, *ID2*, 543 [D470]; Acheson-Sharett conversation, reported in Sharett to Eytan, 5 April 1949, *ID2*, 552 [D477].

5. See, e.g., Kirkbride to Burrows, 6 April 1949 (desp.S1/49), PRO FO371/75349 E4710/1017/31; *FRUS 1949* VI, 751; Touval, *Peace Brokers*, 93; Shlaim, *Collusion*, 436; Pappé, *Making*, 201f.
6. E.g., "Contacts between Arab states regarding Solidarity — Important Meetings in Lebanon and Cairo regarding Palestine problem," *al-Ahram*, 6 Feb. 1949, p.1; Mack to FO, 21 Feb. 1949 (tgm.164), PRO FO371/75347 E2416/1017/31; Pappé, *Making*, 200f.
7. For expressions of this British concern, see material in PRO files FO371/75051 E937/1023/65G; FO371/75330 E1179/1015/31; FO371/75331 papers E1281, E1326, E3053/1015/31; FO371/75334 E8/1016/31; FO371/75335 E930/1016/31G; FO371/75336 E1012, E1273/1016/31; FO371/75337 E1637/1016/31; FO371/75347 papers E2291, E2293, E2359/1017/31; *FRUS 1949* VI, 780f. Cf. Wm. Roger Louis, *The British Empire in the Middle East, 1945-1951: Arab Nationalism, The United States, and Postwar Imperialism*, (Oxford: Clarendon Press, 1984), 566, 568f., 578; Michael Oren, "The Diplomatic Struggle for the Negev, 1946-1956," *Studies in Zionism* 10:2 (Autumn 1989), 205-7. For an expert Israeli appreciation of Egypt-Jordan rivalry over the Negev, see Sasson to Katz, 28 July 1953, ISA 93.02/164/9.
8. Taha al-Hashimi, *Mudhakirat Taha al-Hashimi*, vol.II: 1942-1955 (The Memoirs of Taha al-Hashimi), ed. Khaldun Sati al-Husri (Beirut: 1978), 262 (15 March 1949). For other details of earlier Iraqi maneuvering in the region regarding the Palestine issue, see: Mack (Baghdad) to FO, 7 Jan. 1949, PRO FO371/75334 E340/1016/31G; Dorsz (Baghdad) to USEmb Cairo, 12 Jan. 1949 (tgm.5), WNRC RG84 E/C/G Box207/DF350 Pal(1); Mack to FO, 15 Jan. 1949 (tgm.52), FO371/75330 E717/1015/31G; same to same, 17 Jan. 1949 (tgm.59), FO371/75336 E813/1015/31G; same to same, 20 Jan. 1949 (tgms.75 and 76), FO371/75336 E1008 and E1011/1016/31G; Mack memo, Iraq Palestine policy, 19 Jan. 1949, FO371/75330 E1111/1015/31; *al-Ahram*, 31 Jan. 1949, p.1; Mack to FO, 21 Feb. 1949 (tgm.164), PRO FO371/75347 E2416/1017/31; *ID3*, 221f.; Shlaim, *Collusion*, 467f.
9. Muhammad Khalil, *The Arab States and the Arab League: A Documentary Record*, vol.II International Affairs, (Beirut: Khayats, 1962), 165.
10. Ethridge to Acheson, two tgms. dated 28 Feb. 1949, *FRUS 1949* VI, 776-80.

11. Burdett to Acheson, 2 March 1949, *FRUS 1949* VI, 785f.; Keeley to Acheson, 5 March 1949, ibid., 796-98; Mack to FO, 11 March 1949, PRO FO371/75349 E3638/1017/31.
12. Keeley to Acheson, 5 March 1949, *FRUS 1949* VI, 796-98.
13. Ethridge to Acheson, 14 March 1949, *FRUS 1949* VI, 825f. Cf. Burdett to Acheson, 10 March 1949, ibid., 815; McDonald, *My Mission*, 178.
14. Ahmad al-Shuqayri, *Arba'un Aman fi'l-Hayat al-Arabiyya wa'l-Duliyya* (Forty Years in Arab and International Life), (Beirut: 1969), 308f. No minutes or further firsthand accounts of the Beirut meetings have been found by this researcher. Cf. McDonald, *My Mission*, 178f.
15. Ethridge to Acheson, 22 March 1949, *FRUS 1949* VI, 857.
16. Ethridge and McGhee to Acheson, 22 March 1949, *FRUS 1949* VI, 857-59. On the genesis and operation of the Economic Survey Mission, later headed by Gordon Clapp, see below, pages 43, 76, 104-6.
17. Shuqayri, *Arba'un Aman,* 309f.; report of "second and last joint meeting between commission and Arab states," 5 April, in Ethridge to Acheson, 5 April 1949, *FRUS 1949* VI, 894; Rony E. Gabbay, *A Political Study of the Arab-Jewish Conflict: The Arab Refugee Problem: A Case Study* (Genève: Librairie E. Droz [Paris: Librairie Minard], 1959), 238f.; Azcárate, *Mission*, 149.
18. See, e.g., Acheson to Ethridge, 28 March 1949, *FRUS 1949* VI, 879. The PCC had originally suggested Geneva as the site of the proposed talks.

Chapter 3

1. Ethridge and McGhee to Acheson, 29 March 1949 (tgm.150), USNA 501.BB Pal/3-2949; Ethridge to Acheson, 4 April 1949 (tgm.170), USNA 501.BB Pal/4-449 (cf. *FRUS 1949* VI, 895 n.1); same to same, 5 April 1949, *FRUS 1949* VI, 894; Yalçin remarks, quoted in ibid. 902; Azcárate, *Mission*, 149; Morris, *Birth*, 258f., 275. A completely different picture of Ethridge's mood after the Beirut talks is given in Eytan to Eban, 3 April 1949, *ID2*, 544 [D472].
2. Ethridge to Acheson, 29 March 1949, quoted in Morris, *Birth*, 255.
3. E.g., Azcárate, *Mission*, 145f.; Forsythe, *Peacemaking*, 52.
4. Acheson, memorandum of conversation with Sharett, 5 April 1949, *FRUS 1949* VI, 890-94; Sharett's version of the talk, reported in Sharett to Eytan, 5 April 1949, *ID2*, 552f. [D477]. Cf. Morris, *Birth*, 259; Sharett-Acheson conversation of 22 March, discussed in ibid., 258.
5. Eytan to Shertok, 7 April 1949, *ID2*, 562 [D480]. Another report claimed that the French representative, Claude de Boisanger, later urged the PCC to break off talks with Israel in protest against Ben-Gurion's stand on

Jerusalem. See Comay to Eliash, 29 April 1949, *ID2*, 607 [D525].

6. Unless otherwise indicated, quotations in this and the following paragraphs are taken from Ethridge's report of the meeting of 7 April, in Ethridge to Acheson, 9 April 1949, *FRUS 1949* VI, 902-4, and from the Israeli record of the meeting in *ID2*, 555-62 [D479].
7. Memorandum by the PCC, 11 April 1949 (Doc. IS/9), *ID2*, 567 (handed to M. Comay, Jerusalem). Cf. ibid., 614; *FRUS 1949* VI, 914.
8. Ethridge to Truman, 11 April 1949, *FRUS 1949* VI, 905f. Cf. ibid., 918.
9. Ethridge to Acheson, 13 April 1949, *FRUS 1949* VI, 916.
10. Ethridge report of meeting of 18 April, in Ethridge to Acheson, 20 April 1949, *FRUS 1949* VI, 925-27; Israel State Archives, Yemima Rosenthal (ed.), *Documents on the Foreign Policy of Israel*, vol.4 (May-December 1949) (Jerusalem: 1986), 139 (hereinafter *ID4*); Morris, *Birth*, 262f. I have not located Ben-Gurion's version of this meeting. Cf. *ID2*, 604, 612, 614; *ID4*, 4.
11. E.g., "PCC has Doubts about Jewish Policy," *al-Ahram*, 18 April 1949, p.1; Muhammad Izzat Darwaza, *al-Qadiyya al-Filastiniyya fi Mukhtalif Marahiliha* (The Palestine Cause in its Different Phases), vol.II, (Beirut: 1951 [reprinted 1960]), 254.
12. Ethridge to Acheson, 19 April 1949, quoted in *FRUS 1949* VI, 923 n.1; Burdett to Acheson, 20 April 1949, ibid., 930. Cf. Sharett to Eytan, 16 April 1949, *ID2*, 576 [D495]; Eban to Eytan 19 April 1949, *ID2*, 581 [D499].
13. McClintock draft, 20 April 1949, *FRUS 1949* VI, 927f.
14. Acheson, memorandum of conversation with Elath and Eban, 26 April 1949, *FRUS 1949* VI, 946. Cf. Acheson to USEmb Israel, 28 April 1949, USNA 501.AA/4-2849; *ID2*, 593f.
15. Talk with Satterthwaite and Rockwell, reported in Elath to Sharett, 29 April 1949, *ID2*, 605 [D524]; talk with Webb and Rockwell, in Elath to Sharett, 4 May 1949, *ID4*, 19 [D7]; Acheson to USDel Lausanne, 12 May 1949, *FRUS 1949* VI, 1004.
16. Ethridge to Truman and Acheson, 19 April 1949, *FRUS 1949* VI, 923. Cf. de Boisanger's remarks in Cairo, reported in Patterson to Acheson, 19 Apr. 1949 (A-459), WNRC RG84 E/C/G Box207/DF350 Pal(1); Pappé, *Making*, 202.
17. Acheson to Certain Diplomatic and Consular Offices, 29 April 1949, *FRUS 1949* VI, 959f.
18. Gazit, "Mediation and Mediators," 86. Cf. Eytan, *The First Ten Years*, 63.
19. Meeting with PCC, 24 Feb. 1949, *ID2*, 442f. [D400].

20. Rabinovich, *Road Not Taken*, 55.
21. Consultation meetings, 12 April 1949 (a.m. session and p.m. session), ISA 130.02/2441/7. Extract of Ben-Gurion's comments in *ID2*, 570-72 [D490]. Cf. Eytan to Sharett, 13 April 1949, *ID2*, 572f. [D491]. High-level Israeli consultations were resumed on 19 and 22 April. See ISA 130.02/2447/3 and 130.02/2441/7 (extracts in *ID2*, 585-88 [D505]). Cf. Morris, *Birth*, 261f.; Pappé, *Making*, 201.
22. Shertok comments, meeting with PCC, 24 Feb. 1949, *ID2*, 447-49 [D400]; Sasson to Haykal, 7 April 1949, *ID2*, 563 [D481]; Rabinovich, *Road Not Taken*, 176f.
23. For an account of the Israel-Jordan armistice negotiations at Rhodes and the parallel talks at Shuneh, see: Uri Bar-Joseph, *The Best of Enemies: Israel and Transjordan in the War of 1948*, (London: Frank Cass, 1987), ch.6; Shlaim, *Collusion*, 400-428.
24. Stabler to Acheson, 13 April 1949, *FRUS 1949* VI, 916f. Cf. ibid., 919f., 922; *ID2*, 579f.
25. Burdett to Acheson, 9 April 1949, *FRUS 1949* VI, 905.
26. See, e.g., front-page editorials in the Jordanian daily, *al-Difaa*, 6 and 7 April 1949.
27. *Al-Difaa*, 25 April 1949, p.4; *Falastin*, 28 April 1949, p.1; Pappé, *Making*, 204.
28. Mack to FO, 11 April 1949 (tgm.334), PRO FO371/75349 E4693/1017/31. Cf. *FRUS 1949* VI, 955, 995. In later years, Iraq was said to "pride herself as having never concluded an armistice with Israel." Troutbeck to Eden, 28 Dec. 1953 (desp.213 — 1079/383/53), PRO FO371/111069 VR1072/1.
29. Stabler-Abdallah conversation, reported in Stabler to Acheson, 13 April 1949, *FRUS 1949* VI, 916f.
30. Stabler to Acheson, two telegrams dated 16 April 1949, *FRUS 1949* VI, 919f., 922; Kirkbride to FO, 16 April 1949 (tgm.226), PRO FO371/75349 E4847/1017/31. Cf. Sasson report of the meeting in *ID2*, 579f. [D498]; Shlaim, *Collusion*, 441f.
31. Stabler to Acheson, 16 April 1949, *FRUS 1949* VI, 919f.; Ethridge to Acheson, 20 April 1949, ibid., 924f.
32. "With the August King," *al-Difaa* (editorial), 20 April 1949, p.1; *al-Difaa*, 22 April 1949, pp.1,4; *Falastin*, 22 April 1949, p.1.
33. Dow to FO, 25 April 1949 (tgm.326), PRO FO371/75349 E5203/1017/31.
34. Sharett, note (9 May) of meeting with King Abdallah, Shuneh, 5 May 1949, *ID4*, 33-37 [D15]; Shlaim, *Collusion*, 448-52; Morris, *Birth*, 263f.

35. Shuqayri, *Arba'un Aman,* 310f.; Darwaza, *al-Qadiyya*, 259.
36. See, e.g.: Dow to FO, 20 April 1949 (tgm.318), PRO FO371/75349 E5033/1017/31; *al-Difaa*, 22 April 1949, pp. 1, 4; Dow to FO, 25 April 1949 (tgm.326), FO371/75349 E5203/1017/31.
37. On Hawwari and the other Palestinian refugee delegations, see: Muhammad Nimr al-Hawwari, *Sirr al-Nakba* (The Secret of the Catastrophe), (Nazareth, 1955), 359-75; *ID4*, 12 n.11, 28f., 93, 122f., 359f., 403; Avi Plascov, *The Palestinian Refugees in Jordan, 1948-1957*, (London: Frank Cass, 1981), 20-22, 172f. (nn.62-70); Eytan, *First Ten Years*, 57-59; Gabbay, *A Political Study*, 265-67; Mahdi Abd al-Hadi, *al-Mas'ala al-Filastiniyya wa-Mashari' al-Hulul al-Siyasiyya, 1924-1974* (The Palestinian Question and Plans for Political Solutions), (Beirut: 1975), 163f.; Shlaim, *Collusion*, 489f., 494-96, 503-6; Morris, *Birth*, 264; Pappé, *Making*, 223-25.
38. Abd al-Hadi, *al-Mas'ala*, 136.
39. Record of Meeting Held Between Palestinian Arabs from the Triangle Area and Representatives of Israel near Mandelbaum Gate at 1500 hours on 27 April 1949, ISA 130.16/2948/7; Dow to FO, 20 April 1949 (tgm.318), PRO FO371/75349 E5033/1017/31; Stabler to Acheson, 15 April 1949, quoted in *FRUS 1949* VI, 917 n.2.

Chapter 4

1. See, e.g., *FRUS 1949* VI, 990-92, 1013-15, 1064f., 1086f., 1108f.; *ID2*, 615; *ID4*, 13; George McGhee, *Envoy to the Middle World: Adventures in Diplomacy*, fwd. Dean Rusk, (New York: Harper & Row, 1983), chap. 4; Morris, *Birth*, 260; Pappé, *Making*, 219f. (which erroneously has McGhee visiting Lausanne).
2. Eban to Hirsch, 29 April 1949, *ID2*, 603 [D521].
3. The account of this meeting is based on: Hirsch to Sharett, 27 April 1949, *ID2*, 598 [D515]; Ethridge to Acheson, 28 April 1949, *FRUS 1949* VI, 955. In this and the following chapters, PCC meetings have been reconstructed from available accounts of the various participants. The official PCC Summary Records of these meetings, labeled "Restricted" distribution, are still classified at the UNA and are not open to historical researchers. Most of the Israel-PCC meetings and correspondence surrounding the Lausanne Conference are in ISA 130.02/2441/1, /2, /9, /10, /11 and 130.02/2442/5-8. Occasional records of individual meetings and memoranda have found their way into miscellaneous US State Department and British Foreign Office files, which are open to scholars.

4. Eytan to Sharett, 30 April 1949, *ID2*, 616 [D526]; same to same, 3 May 1949, *ID4*, 11f. [D4]; Morris, *Birth*, 263. Press statement of 30 April 1949, quoted in: *ID5*, 224; *ID4*, 26 n.1; Cf. draft in Sharett to Hirsch, 28 April 1949, *ID2*, 601 [D517]; *ha-Aretz*, 2 May 1949 (transcript in ISA 130.02/2446/6a); *FRUS 1949* VI, 975 n.3.
5. Ethridge to Acheson, 4 May 1949, *FRUS 1949* VI, 975. Cf. Morris, *Birth*, 262, 265.
6. *FRUS 1949* VI, 956. Cf. *al-Ahram*, 29 April 1949, p.1; Shuqayri, *Arba'un Aman*, 311.
7. Abd al-Mun'im Mustafa, quoted in *al-Difaa*, 1 May 1949, p.1. Cf. sources cited in note 27, Chap. 3; Azcárate, *Mission*, 149.
8. Eytan to Sharett, 9 May 1949, *ID4*, 31 [D13]. Cf. Hawwari's similar observations, *Sirr al-Nakba*, 359f.
9. Ethridge to Acheson, 4 May 1949, *FRUS 1949* VI, 975.
10. Vincent to Acheson, 3 May 1949, *FRUS 1949* VI, 968f.; Eytan to Sharett, 30 April 1949, *ID2*, 613f. [D526]; Ethridge to Acheson, 9 May 1949, *FRUS 1949* VI, 989. Cf. UN Conciliation Commission for Palestine, *Third Progress Report* [UN Doc. A/927, 21 June, 1949], para. 3 (cited hereinafter as PCC, *Third Progress Rpt.*); *ID4*, 70; *FRUS 1949* VI, 1069f.; Morris, *Birth*, 263.
11. Eban statement, enclosed in Eytan to Ethridge, 4 May 1949, *ID4*, 14-16 [D5]. Cf. Acheson to Ethridge, 4 May 1949, *FRUS 1949* VI, 979; Morris, *Birth*, 264.
12. Elath remarks to Webb, reported in Elath to Sharett, 4 May 1949, *ID4*, 19 [D7].
13. PCC, Summary Record of 50th Meeting (Lausanne), 6 May 1949 [SR/50], copy in USNA 501.BB Pal/5-2349.
14. Eytan to Ethridge, 6 May 1949, *ID4*, 26f. [D10]; Ethridge to Acheson, 10 May 1949, *FRUS 1949* VI, 992f.; PCC Doc. IS/16, *ID4*, 60.
15. Elath to Acheson, 11 May 1949, *FRUS 1949* VI, 996-98 and *ID4*, 39-41 [D18].
16. PCC (Ethridge) to Acheson, 12 May 1949, *FRUS 1949* VI, 1003.
17. Quoted in Eytan to Sharett, 14 May 1949, *ID4*, 51 [D26]. Cf. Pappé, *Making*, 209.
18. E.g., Eytan, *First Ten Years*, 54.
19. E.g., "a forum regulated by agreed rules of procedure at which representatives of sovereign states (or of groups aspiring to that status) meet, ostensibly to settle points of dispute, following previous hostility, within the framework of formal negotiations." R. Cohen and S. Cohen, *Peace Conferences: The Formal Aspects* (Leonard Davis

Institute: Jerusalem Papers on Peace Problems, Jan. 1974), 5.

20. *ID2*, 604f.; *ID4*, 23. Cf. *ID2*, 603; *ID4*, 6; *ha-Aretz*, 2 May 1949.
21. *Ha-Aretz*, 28 April 1949, quoted in Ruth Levy Ninberg, *ha-Emda ha-Aravit Klapei Ve'idat Lausanne, 1949* [The Arab Position at the Lausanne Conference], unpublished M.A. thesis, (University of Haifa, November 1987), 67.
22. Shlaim, *Collusion*, 476.
23. For first-hand Israeli reports of such meetings, see *ID4*, 11f., 23 n.8, 28f., 82f., 86, 89, 93, 120, 121 n.1, 126, 149, 177, 191f., 203, 256, 266, 271f., 280f., 286f., 293, 300f., 334f., 357f., 380f., 390f., 403, 445f. Cf. Eytan, *First Ten Years*, 54; Shlaim, *Collusion*, 476-82 (Israel-Jordan), 483-88 (Israel-Egypt), ch.16 *passim* (Israel-Palestinians); Rabinovich, *Road Not Taken*, 61-63, 177-84.
24. Forsythe, *Peacemaking*, 48 n.36; Hirsch to Sharett, 1 May 1949, *ID4*, 6 [D1]; Shlaim, *Collusion*, 469.
25. See, e.g., Pappé, *Making*, 221f.
26. Pappé, *Making*, 206; but cf. ibid., 222, 233f.
27. PCC, Summary Record of 50th Meeting (Lausanne), 6 May 1949 [SR/50], copy in USNA 501.BB Pal/5-2349. Cf. *ID4*, 31; PCC, *Third Progress Rpt.*, paras. 6-8; Darwaza, *al-Qadiyya*, 254; Pappé, *Making*, 205f.
28. PCC, Summary Record of 50th Mtg (Lausanne), 6 May 1949 [SR/50], loc.cit.; Benjamin Shwadran, "Palestine Conciliation Commission," *Middle Eastern Affairs* (Oct. 1950), 280f. For a slightly different presentation of Lausanne procedures, see Pappé, *Making*, 204f. This researcher has seen no evidence to warrant Pappé's claim (p.205) that the commissioners "did not limit themselves to passing the demands of one party to the other, but also tabled their own proposals."
29. Ethridge to Acheson, 9 May 1949, *FRUS 1949* VI, 988.

Chapter 5

1. Ethridge to Acheson, 10 May 1949, *FRUS 1949* VI, 993f.; ibid., 969; Eytan to Ethridge, 4 May 1949, *ID4*, 17-19 [D6]; PCC, Summary Record of 50th Meeting (Lausanne), 6 May 1949 [SR/50], copy in USNA 501.BB Pal/5-2349; Eytan to Sharett, 3 May 1949, *ID4*, 12 [D4]; Azcárate, *Mission*, 150; Pappé, *Making*, 207.
2. On the other hand, one UN official in Damascus felt that, given Husni Za'im's secret offer to settle Palestinian refugees on Syrian territory, Israel might benefit from a constructive Syrian attitude on the refugee question at Lausanne if it succeeded in reaching a breakthrough in the stalled armistice talks. See: Vigier to Bunche, 11 May 1949 (tgm. DA-16),

UNA DAG-13/3.3.0:20. Cf. Avi Shlaim, "Husni Za'im and the Plan to Resettle Palestinian Refugees in Syria," *Jnl. of Palestine Studies* 15:4 [no. 60] (Summer 1986), 68-80; Rabinovich, *Road Not Taken*, ch.3.

3. Eytan to de Boisanger, 9 May 1949, quoted in *ID4* Companion Volume, 11; Eytan to Sharett, 9 May 1949, *ID4*, 29f. [D13]; Eytan to Azcárate, 11 June 1949, *ID4*, 118-20 [D71]; Ethridge to Acheson, 12 May 1949, *FRUS 1949* VI, 998. Cf. *ID4*, 50, 124, 162f.; Shuqayri, *Arba'un Aman*, 311; Khouri, "United Nations Peace Efforts," 35; Shlaim, *Collusion*, 470.
4. Eytan to Sharett, 13 June 1949, *ID4*, 124 [D74]; Akram Zuaytir, *al-Qadiyya al-Filastiniyya* (The Palestine Cause), (?Cairo: 1955), 246; Rabinovich, *Road Not Taken*, 57; Pappé, *Making*, 208, 212.
5. UN Doc.A/927, 21 June 1949, Annex A. Text reproduced in John Norton Moore, ed., *The Arab-Israeli Conflict*, vol.III Documents, (Princeton: Princeton University Press, 1974), 493f.; *ID4*, 50f.
6. Azcárate, *Mission*, 150.
7. Eytan, *The First Ten Years*, 60; Eytan remarks, quoted in Nicholls (Tel Aviv) to Shuckburgh, 31 Oct. 1955 (desp. 1031/107/55), PRO FO371/115880 VR1076/329; Shlaim, *Collusion*, 469f.
8. Eban to Sharett, 15 June 1949, *ID4*, 133 [D79]. Cf. Eban to Eytan, 8 June 1949, *ID4*, 105 [D63].
9. Pappé, *Making*, 212.
10. Israel Office of Information, *Israel's Struggle for Peace*, (New York: 1960), 50.
11. Shuqayri, *Arba'un Aman*, 311f.
12. See, e.g., comments by Fuad Ammoun, quoted in Chapman-Andrews to FO, 18 Aug. 1951 (tgm.456), PRO FO371/91365 EE1071/13; Azcárate, *Mission*, 150f.; Zuaytir, *al-Qadiyya*, 247; Darwaza, *al-Qadiyya*, 251f.; Pappé, *Making*, 235, 298 n.85.
13. See, e.g., Zuaytir, *al-Qadiyya*, 245.
14. E.g., Abd al-Munim Mustafa in February 1950 (see Rabinovich, *Road Not Taken*, 186); Ali Mahir, quoted in Stevenson (Cairo) to Bowker, 14 Nov. 1952 (desp. 1072/27/52), PRO FO371/98479 EE1073/94; Lebanese politicians in late 1955, as reported in: Scott (Beirut) to FO, 3 Oct. 1955 (tgm. 731), PRO FO371/115880 VR1076/320; Emmerson (Beirut) to USSD, 17 Oct. 1955 (tgm. 441), USNA NEA Lot59 D518 Box30; same to same, 17 Nov. 1955 (tgm. 559), loc.cit. Box31.
15. Shuqayri, *Arba'un Aman*, 313. Cf. Pappé, *Making*, 208f. (quoting Egyptian historian Salah al-Aqad and Syrian Foreign Minister Adil Arslan), 210f.; Forsythe, *Peacemaking*, 50f.; Khouri, "United Nations Peace Efforts," 31f., 35f.

16. Eytan to Sharett, 9 May 1949, *ID4*, 30 [D13].
17. See, e.g., Webb, memorandum of conversation with Egyptian ambassador, 10 June 1949, USNA 501.BB Pal/6-1049; also reported in Webb to USEmb Cairo, 11 June 1949, *FRUS 1949* VI, 1115-17.
18. See, e.g., *Falastin*, 18 May 1949, p.1; Patterson to Acheson, 17 May 1949 (A-574), WNRC RG84 E/C/G Box207/DF350 Pal(1).
19. *FRUS 1949* VI, 999; Shuqayri, *Arba'un Aman*, 312f.; Gabbay, *Political Study*, 247; Azcárate, *Mission*, 153f.; Forsythe, *Peacemaking*, 58; Zuaytir, *al-Qadiyya*, 248.
20. Eytan to Sharett, 14 May 1949, *ID4*, 51 [D26]; Ethridge to Acheson, 20 May 1949, *FRUS 1949* VI, 1036-38; Eytan to Sharett, 21 May 1949, *ID4*, 58f. [D32]; Shlaim, *Collusion*, 470; Pappé, *Making*, 212.
21. Arab delegations memorandum (Doc. AR/8), 18 May 1949, copies in PRO FO371/75350 E7857/1017/31 and ISA 130.02/2441/9.
22. Arab delegations memorandum to PCC (Doc. AR/11), 21 May 1949, copy in PRO FO371/75350 E7857/1017/31. Cf. Shuqayri, *Arba'un Aman*, 314; Hawwari, *Sirr al-Nakba*, 363; *FRUS 1949* VI, 1043; PCC, *Eighth Progress Rpt.*, extract in Meron Medzini, ed., *Israel's Foreign Relations: Selected Documents 1947-1974*, (Jerusalem: Ministry of Foreign Affairs, 1976), 276.
23. Eytan to de Boisanger, 25 May 1949, *ID4*, 60f. [D34]. Cf. *FRUS 1949* VI, 1065-67; Morris, *Birth*, 255.
24. Eytan to de Boisanger, 25 May 1949, *ID4*, 64f. [D35]. Cf. *FRUS 1949* VI, 1067f.
25. Eytan to Sharett, 21 May 1949, *ID4*, 58f. [D32].
26. Eytan to Kidron, 23 Feb. 1955, ISA 130.02/2410/10 (emphasis added).
27. Ethridge to Acheson, 20 May 1949, *FRUS 1949* VI, 1036-38; Pappé, *Making*, 215.
28. Ethridge to Acheson, 28 May 1949, *FRUS 1949* VI, 1067. Cf. *ID4*, 63 n.3.
29. Eytan to Sharett, 27 May 1949, *ID4*, 70 [D37].
30. Eytan to de Boisanger, 31 May 1949, *ID4*, 79f. [D44]. Cf. PCC, *Eighth Progress Rpt.*, extract in Medzini, *Israel's Foreign Relations*, 276f.
31. Sasson and Liff to Sharett, 31 May 1949, *ID4*, 82f. [D46].
32. Ethridge to Acheson, 28 May 1949, *FRUS 1949* VI, 1071f. Cf. remarks of Abd al-Rahman Azzam, reported in Patterson to Acheson, 19 July 1949 (tgm.689), USNA 501.MA Pal/7-1949; Rabinovich, *Road Not Taken*, 62; Shlaim, *Collusion*, 432f., 478f.; Bar-Joseph, *Best of Enemies*, ch.6.

Chapter 6

1. Truman note to Ben-Gurion, in Webb to USEmb Israel, 28 May 1949, *FRUS 1949* VI, 1072-74. Cf. ibid., 1074f.; *ID4*, 75-77; Ben-Gurion Diary, 29 May 1949, BGA (transl. in Tom Segev, *1949: The First Israelis*, (New York/London: Free Press/Collier Macmillan, 1986), 35f.); McDonald, *My Mission*, ch.xvi; Forsythe, *Peacemaking*, 52f.; Khouri, "United Nations Peace Efforts," 37f.; Shlaim, *Collusion*, 471f.; Morris, *Birth*, 265; Pappé, *Making*, 218f.
2. McDonald, *My Mission*, 184. Cf. *FRUS 1949* VI, 1102-6, 1148-53, 1168-77; *ID4*, 107-11, 168-76.
3. Darwaza, *al-Qadiyya*, 254-58.
4. Ethridge to Acheson, 28 May 1949, *FRUS 1949* VI, 1069-71.
5. Eytan to de Boisanger, 29 May 1949, *ID4*, 74f. [D41]; Mordechai Gazit, "Ben-Gurion's 1949 Proposal to Incorporate the Gaza Strip with Israel," *Studies in Zionism* 8:2 (1987), 230; Morris, *Birth*, 269.
6. Gazit, "Ben-Gurion's 1949 Proposal," 228-30.
7. On the tactical considerations behind Israel's Gaza offer, see: Gabbay, *Political Study*, 244-46; Gazit, "Ben-Gurion's 1949 Proposal," 225-28; Morris, *Birth*, 266-71.
8. Ethridge-Ben-Gurion talk (18 April), reported in Ethridge to Acheson, 20 April 1949, *FRUS 1949* VI, 926-27; Morris, *Birth*, 267; Gazit, "Ben-Gurion's 1949 Proposal," 226.
9. Consultation meeting, IMFA, 22 April 1949, ISA 130.02/2441/7 (extract in *ID2*, 587f. [D505]). Cf. *FRUS 1949* VI, 1076, 1104, 1111, 1116 n.2, 1124, 1175; Jackson, minute for Bevin, 16 June 1949, FO371/75333 E7648/1015/31G; Morris, *Birth*, 268; Shlaim, *Collusion*, 470. While this researcher follows Mordechai Gazit ("Ben-Gurion's 1949 Proposal") in attributing the idea to Ben-Gurion, Ilan Pappé (basing himself on an editorial note in *ID4*, 10) treats it as "The Gaza Proposal of Mark Ethridge" (*Making*, 213).
10. Eytan to Sharett, 30 April 1949, *ID2*, 615 [D526].
11. *ID4*, 10. Cf. *FRUS 1949* VI, 1076; Morris, *Birth*, 268f.
12. Eytan to Sharett, 21 May 1949, *ID4*, 58f. [D32]; Ethridge to Acheson, 20 May 1949, *FRUS 1949* VI, 1036; same to same, 28 May 1949, ibid., 1070f.
13. Eytan to de Boisanger, 29 May 1949, *ID4*, 74f. [D41]; Gazit, "Ben-Gurion's 1949 Proposal," 230; Morris, *Birth*, 269.
14. PCC, *Eighth Progress Rpt.*, extract in Medzini, *Israel's Foreign Relations*, 277. Cf. Gabbay, *Political Study*, 245f.; Hawwari, *Sirr al-Nakba*, 363; Darwaza, *al-Qadiyya*, 252; Forsythe, *Peacemaking*, 54 n.61.

15. Eytan to de Boisanger, 31 May 1949, *ID4*, 80 [D44].
16. Morris, *Birth*, 266.
17. Webb to USDel Lausanne, 4 June 1949, *FRUS 1949* VI, 1090; Webb to USEmb Israel, 8 June 1949, ibid., 1096; Morris, *Birth*, 269; Gazit, "Ben-Gurion's 1949 Proposal," 231.
18. Webb to USDel Lausanne, 4 June 1949, *FRUS 1949* VI, 1090f.; Morris, *Birth*, 269; Gazit, "Ben-Gurion's 1949 Proposal," 232.
19. Ethridge to Acheson, 12 June 1949, *FRUS 1949* VI, 1125. Cf. Morris, *Birth*, 265, 269, 271, 276.
20. E.g., M. Comay views, reported in Franks to FO, 21 April 1949 (tgm.2283), PRO FO371/75349 E5065/1017/31; Ethridge to Acheson, 9 May 1949, *FRUS 1949* VI, 989; Herlitz-McDonald conversation (30 May), reported in McDonald to Acheson, 31 May 1949, ibid., 1076; Morris, *Birth*, 268.
21. Ethridge to Acheson, 9 May 1949, *FRUS 1949* VI, 989.
22. Sasson to Sharett, 1 June 1949, *ID4*, 86 [D48]; Morris, *Birth*, 271. Cf. Rabinovich, *Road Not Taken*, 178f.; Mustafa remarks (17 July), reported in Patterson to Acheson, 19 July 1949 (tgm.689), USNA 501.MA Pal/7-1949.
23. See: Sasson to Sharett, 11 June 1949, *ID4*, 120 [D72]; Eytan to Sharett, 15 June 1949, discussed in *ID4*, 126 n.16; Rabinovich, *Road Not Taken*, 178f.
24. Campbell to FO, 6 May 1949 (tgm.649), FO371/75333 E5713/1015/31G; Campbell-Patterson talk, reported in Patterson to Acheson, 19 July 1949 (tgm.689), USNA 501.MA Pal/7-1949. See also: Abu al-Huda talk with Khashaba, reported in Kirkbride to Bevin, 21 April 1949 (desp.28; S143/49), PRO FO371/75332 E5395/1015/31; Jackson, minute for Bevin, 16 June 1949, FO371/75333 E7648/1015/31G; Troutbeck to FO, 16 July 1949 (tgm.346), PRO FO371/75350 E8704/1017/31; Morris, *Birth*, 273; Pappé, *Making*, 216f.
25. Webb, memorandum of conversation, 10 June 1949, USNA 501.BB Pal/6-1049; Webb to USEmb Cairo, 11 June 1949, *FRUS 1949* VI, 1115-17; Gazit, "Ben-Gurion's 1949 Proposal," 232; Morris, *Birth*, 271.
26. Acheson to USEmb UK, 25 June 1949, *FRUS 1949* VI, 1180. Cf. Patterson to Acheson, 14 June 1949, quoted in ibid., 1117 n.4.
27. PCC meeting with Arab delegations (25 June), reported in Hare to Acheson, 27 June 1949, *FRUS 1949* VI, 1186f.
28. Ethridge memorandum to Rusk, 15 June 1949, *FRUS 1949* VI, 1139. Cf. Eban to Sharett, 17 June 1949, *ID4*, 140 [D84]; same to same, 18 June 1949 and same to same, 20 June 1949, both discussed in *ID4*, 140 n.12;

Morris, *Birth*, 276; McGhee, *Envoy*, 36.

29. US Govt., *aide-mémoire* to Israel Govt., 24 June 1949, *FRUS 1949* VI, 1175; Rusk, memorandum of conversation with U. Heyd, 24 [erroneously given as 25] June 1949, ibid., 1177f.; Heyd to Sharett, 24 June 1949, discussed in *ID4*, 172 (Editorial note); Rusk talk with Heyd, 28 June, reported in Acheson to USEmb Israel, 1 July 1949, *FRUS 1949* VI, 1196; Gazit, "Ben-Gurion's 1949 Proposal," 234; Morris, *Birth*, 271f., 273; Rabinovich, *Road Not Taken*, 179f.
30. Acheson to USEmb UK, 25 June 1949, *FRUS 1949* VI, 1179f.; Gazit, "Ben-Gurion's 1949 Proposal," 234f.; Morris, *Birth*, 272f.
31. Jackson, minute for Bevin, 16 June 1949, PRO FO371/75333 E7648/1015/31G.
32. Douglas (London) to Acheson, 28 June 1949 (tgm. 2501), USNA 501.MA Pal/6-2849; cf. *FRUS 1949* VI, 1180 n.3; Gazit, "Ben-Gurion's 1949 Proposal," 234.
33. Acheson to USEmb UK, 30 June 1949, *FRUS 1949* VI, 1191-93; Gazit, "Ben-Gurion's 1949 Proposal," 235f.
34. Acheson to USEmb Egypt, 25 June 1949, *FRUS 1949* VI, 1181f.
35. Patterson to Acheson, 27 June 1949, *FRUS 1949* VI, 1188f.; Gazit, "Ben-Gurion's 1949 Proposal," 235.
36. Acheson to USEmb Egypt, 28 June 1949, *FRUS 1949* VI, 1191.

Chapter 7

1. Beirut meetings (8-12 June), in Strang report on tour of Middle East, 4 July 1949, para.50, PRO FO371/75067 E8752/1052/65; Vigier to Bunche, 1 June 1949 (tgm.DA-52), UNA DAG-13/3.3.0:20.
2. Eytan to Sharett, 13 June 1949, *ID4*, 121 [D74].
3. Ethridge to Acheson, 10 June 1949, *FRUS 1949* VI, 1112-14. Cf. Eytan's comments on the meeting in *ID4*, 123 [D74].
4. Eytan to Sharett, 13 June 1949, *ID4*, 122 [D74]; Ethridge to Acheson, 10 June 1949, *FRUS 1949* VI, 1112; Morris, *Birth*, 265. For the PCC secretary's views of Arab demands as "curious" and unrealistic, see Azcárate, *Mission*, 151.
5. Eytan to Sharett, 13 June 1949, *ID4*, 123-25 [D74]; Hare to Acheson, 12 June 1949, *FRUS 1949* VI, 1122f.; Gabbay, *Political Study*, 246f. Cf. Eytan to Azcárate, 11 June 1949, *ID4*, 118-20 [D71].
6. Eytan to Eban, 13 June 1949, *ID4*, 128f. [D75].
7. Hare's account of PCC meeting of 13 June, in Hare to Acheson, 14 June 1949, *FRUS 1949* VI, 1135f.
8. Hare's account of meeting of 14 June, in Hare to Acheson, 15 June 1949,

FRUS 1949 VI, 1142f.

9. Eytan to Azcárate, 19 June 1949, *ID4*, 140f. [D85]; same to same, 20 June 1949, *ID4*, 141f. [D86]; same to same, 23 June 1949, *ID4*, 152f. [D95]; Shlaim, *Collusion*, 501f.
10. Eytan to Azcárate, 27 June 1949, *ID4*, 178-80 [D108].
11. Shuqayri, *Arba'un Aman*, 314. Eytan was, in fact, deliberately bombarding the PCC with memoranda. See, e.g., *ID4*, 126, 129.
12. Full Eng. transl. of the speech in: PRO FO371/75199 E8639/1023/131 and CZA A245/35/I; extracts in Medzini, *Israel's Foreign Relations*, 273-76; Heb. in Moshe Sharett, *Be-Shaar ha-Umot, 1946-1949* [At the Gate of the Nations], (Tel Aviv: Am Oved, 1958), 360-75.
13. Hare's report of PCC meeting, in Hare to Acheson, 17 June 1949, *FRUS 1949* VI, 1154f.; same to same, 20 June 1949 (tgm.974), USNA 501.BB Pal/6-2049.
14. Hare report of meeting of 25 June, in Hare to Acheson, 27 June 1949, *FRUS 1949* VI, 1186f.
15. Webb to Hare, 18 June 1949, *FRUS 1949* VI, 1155; Ethridge memorandum to Rusk, 15 June 1949, ibid., 1137-39; *ID4*, 164f.
16. Hare to Acheson, 20 June 1949 (tgm.974, PALUN.220), USNA 501.BB Pal/6-2049. Cf. Warner (Geneva) to Chadwick, 21 June 1949, (desp.103/91/49), PRO FO371/75350 E7857/1017/31.
17. Ethridge to Acheson, 12 June 1949, *FRUS 1949* VI, 1124f.; Morris, *Birth*, 276; Pappé, *Making*, 229, 241.
18. PCC, *Third Progress Rpt.*, paras.12-38.

Chapter 8

1. Webb to Acheson (Paris), 12 June 1949, *FRUS 1949* VI, 1126.
2. Hare to Acheson, 20 June 1949 (tgm.974), USNA 501.BB Pal/6-2049. Cf. *FRUS 1949* VI, 1155 n.1.
3. McGhee memorandum for Acheson, 13 July 1949, *FRUS 1949* VI, 1218-21. Cf. Acheson to USDel Lausanne, 26 July 1949, ibid., 1257f.
4. Acheson to USEmb France, 12 July 1949, *FRUS 1949* VI, 1217f. The latter phrase was directed especially to the Arab governments. Cf. Acheson to Certain Diplomatic Offices [Cairo, Tel Aviv, etc.], 16 July 1949, ibid., 1230f.; editorial note, ibid., 1239f.
5. See, e.g., Keeley to Acheson, 18 July 1949, *FRUS 1949* VI, 1234; Stabler to Acheson, 23 July 1949 (tgm.289), USNA 501.BB Pal/7-2349; Forsythe, *Peacemaking*, 55.
6. *ID4*, 206 (Editorial note); Sharett to Eban, 6 July 1949, *ID4*, 207 [D124]. Cf. *ID4*, 221.

7. Text of announcement in Hirsch to Azcárate, 8 July 1949, *ID4*, 208-10 [D126]. Cf. Sharett speech, 15 June 1949 (note 12, Chap. 7 above); IMFA consultation, 13 July 1949, *ID4*, 220f. [D136].
8. Acheson to USEmb Israel, 11 July 1949, *FRUS 1949* VI, 1217. For a critical presentation of the family-reunion scheme, see Morris, *Birth*, 277f.
9. Keeley to Acheson, 18 July 1949, *FRUS 1949* VI, 1234.
10. Acheson to Keeley, 20 July 1949, discussed in *FRUS 1949* VI, 1235 n.3; Rabinovich, *Road Not Taken*, 82-91.
11. Stabler to Acheson, 23 July 1949 (tgm.289), quoted in *FRUS 1949* VI, 1231 n.2.
12. Sharett to Eytan, 29 June 1949, summarized in *ID4*, 186 n.1; Eban to Eytan, 8 June 1949, *ID4*, 101 [D63]; Morris, *Birth*, 272.
13. Eytan to Sharett, 30 June 1949, *ID4*, 186-89 [D111]. Unless otherwise indicated, quotations in this and the following paragraph are from this letter.
14. Heyd to Sharett, 24 June 1949, quoted in *ID4*, 172 (Editorial note).
15. On the importance of Eilat, see, e.g., Ben-Gurion's views quoted in Bar-Joseph, *Best of Enemies*, 206.
16. Sasson to Sharett, 3 July 1949, *ID4*, 203 [D120].
17. Acheson to USEmb Egypt, 1 July 1949, *FRUS 1949* VI, 1195.
18. Eban to Sharett, 4 July 1949, *ID4*, 204 [D122]. Cf. same to Shiloah, 28 July 1949, *ID4*, 259 [D158].
19. Eban to McGhee, 8 July 1949, *ID4*, 212f. [D129].
20. Hassuna, as reported in Patterson to Acheson, 7 July 1949 (tgm.649), USNA 867N.01/7-749, quoted in *FRUS 1949* VI, 1195 n.2.
21. Patterson to Acheson, 19 July 1949 (tgm.689), USNA 501.MA Pal/7-1949 (cf. *FRUS 1949* VI, 1243 n.1).
22. Lourie and Rafael to Sharett, 12 July 1949, *ID4*, 218 [D134]. See also conversation with McGhee and Hare, reported in Eban to Sharett, 8 July 1949, *ID4*, 211 [D128]; Sharett, address at political consultation, IMFA, 13 July 1949, *ID4*, 223 [D137].
23. See, e.g., Eytan to Sharett, 3 May 1949, *ID4*, 13 [D4]; Ben-Gurion, *Yoman ha-Milhama*, 993 (14 July 1949); Comay to Eliash, 10 Jan. 1950, ISA 130.02/2593/12; McDonald, *My Mission*, 183; Morris, *Birth*, 271.
24. Eban-Rafael talk with Ross, reported in Eban to Sharett, 6 July 1949, *ID4*, 209 [D125]; Acheson to USEmb Egypt, 1 July 1949, *FRUS 1949* VI, 1195; ibid., 1209 n.2; Hare-Bromley talk (8 July), reported in UKChancery Washington to Eastern Dept. FO, 12 July 1949 (desp.55/89/49), PRO FO371/75350 E8707/1017/31.

25. Patterson to Acheson, 7 July 1949 (tgm.649), USNA 867N.01/7-749, quoted in *FRUS 1949* VI, 1195 n.2.
26. Acheson to USEmb Egypt, 14 July 1949, *FRUS 1949* VI, 1228f. Cf. Sharett to Elath, 21 July 1949, *ID4*, 238 [D144].
27. Acheson to USEmb UK, 14 July 1949 (tgm.2450), USNA 501.BB Pal/7-1449.
28. Wright-Douglas talk (14 July), reported in Douglas to Acheson, 15 [?14] July 1949 (tgm.2790), USNA 501.BB Pal/7-1549 (cf. *FRUS 1949* VI, 1229 n.4); FO to Washington, 23 July 1949 (tgm.7309), PRO FO371/75350 E8789/1017/31; Acheson to USEmb Israel, 10 Aug. 1949 (tgm.510), USNA 501.BB Pal/8-149.
29. Eban to Sharett, 6 July 1949, *ID4*, 208 [D125]. Cf. *FRUS 1949* VI, 1213 n.1.
30. Acheson to Austin, 8 July 1949, *FRUS 1949* VI, 1213; Morris, *Birth*, 272.
31. Hare, memorandum of conversation (Eban-Heyd-McGhee), 7 July 1949, *FRUS 1949* VI, 1208f.; Morris, *Birth*, 271f.
32. See, e.g., Troutbeck to FO, 16 July 1949 (tgm.346), PRO FO371/75350 E8704/1017/31; Morris, *Birth*, 271, 273.
33. Mayall to Clutton, 19 July 1949 (desp.169/131/49), PRO FO371/75351 E9059/1017/31. Cf. Patterson to Acheson, 19 July 1949, discussed below; Morris, *Birth*, 273f.
34. Patterson to Acheson, 19 July 1949 (tgm.689), USNA 501.MA Pal/7-1949 (cf. *FRUS 1949* VI, 1243 n.1). The telegram summarizes Patterson's conversations with Hasan Yusuf, Khashaba, Fahmy Bey, Azzam, and Abd al-Mun'im Mustafa. Quotations in this and the following paragraphs are from this telegram. Cf. Gazit, "Ben-Gurion's 1949 Proposal," 237.
35. Cf. Wright, note of talk with Hare, 1 July 1949, PRO FO371/75350 E8393/1017/31; Jackson minute, 4 July 1949, FO371/75350 E8274/1017/31; Morris, *Birth*, 271, 273f.
36. Mayall to Clutton, 19 July 1949 (desp.169/131/49), PRO FO371/75351 E9059/1017/31; Patterson to Acheson, 19 July 1949 (n.30).
37. Sharett, guidelines for Lausanne delegation, 25 July 1949, *ID4*, 246 [D146]; Morris, *Birth*, 274f.; Shlaim, *Collusion*, 502f. Cf. Elath remarks, quoted in *FRUS 1949* VI, 1264; Rabinovich, *Road Not Taken*, 180f.; Pappé, *Making*, 217.
38. Acheson to USDel Lausanne, 22 July 1949, *FRUS 1949* VI, 1243f.
39. Rockwell to Acheson, 20 July 1949, *FRUS 1949* VI, 1239; Shiloah to Sharett, 31 July 1949, *ID4*, 268 [D164]; Morris, *Birth*, 274. Israeli representatives were following instructions to avoid raising the Gaza question for the time being, allowing the impression to be formed that

"Israel did not particularly care" whether the strip remained in Egyptian hands. Sharett to Sasson, 28 July 1949, discussed in *ID4*, 256 n.4. Cf. *ID4*, 245.

40. Summary of Egyptian *aide-mémoire* handed to Patterson (25 July) in Patterson to Acheson, 26 July 1949 (tgm.713), USNA 501.MA Pal/7-2649.
41. Acheson to USEmb Egypt, 4 August 1949 (tgm.778), USNA 501.MA Pal/7-2649; cf. *FRUS 1949* VI, 1244 n.3; Gazit, "Ben-Gurion's 1949 Proposal," 238.
42. Elath to Sharett, 25 July 1949, *ID4*, 247 [D147]; McGhee-Elath conversation, 25 July 1949, quoted in editorial note, *FRUS 1949* VI, 1248. Cf. Eban to Shiloah, 28 July 1949, *ID4*, 259 [D158].
43. See, e.g., Eban to Sharett, 27 July 1949, *ID4*, 257 [D156]; Wilkins-Elath conversation, reported in Elath to Sharett, 28 July 1949, *ID4*, 263 [D160]; Rusk, memorandum of conversation (Elath-Heyd-McGhee-Wilkins), 28 July 1949, *FRUS 1949* VI, 1264; Sasson-Rockwell talk (24 Aug.), reported in Sasson to Sharett, 25 Aug. 1949, *ID4*, 394 [D241]; Patterson-Hassuna talk (19 Sept.), reported in Patterson to Acheson, 19 Sept. 1949 (airgm.A-1000), USNA 501.BB Pal/9-1949; McGhee views expressed at Istanbul consultations, as reported by McDonald, and Ben-Gurion remarks to McDonald, both in Comay to Elath, 5 Dec. 1949, *ID4*, 684f. [D460]; Rabinovich, *Road Not Taken*, 188f.
44. See, e.g., Eliash-Helm talk, reported in Eliash to Sharett, 5 Aug. 1949, *ID4*, 292f. [D183]; Sharett to Shiloah and Sasson, 9 Aug. 1949, *ID4*, 304f. [D192].
45. See, e.g., Sasson to Sharett, 4 Aug. 1949, *ID4*, 286f. [D178]; Sasson and Shiloah to Sharett, 21 Aug. 1949, *ID4*, 381 [D232]; Gazit, "Ben-Gurion's 1949 Proposal," 241; Shlaim, *Collusion*, 485-87.
46. Varda Shiffer, "The 1949 Israeli Offer to Repatriate 100,000 Palestinian Refugees," *Middle East Focus* 9:2 (Fall 1986), 14, 18.
47. Wright, note of talk with Hare, 1 July 1949, PRO FO371/75350 E8393/1017/31.
48. Strang, Report to Secretary of State, 4 July 1949, PRO FO371/75067 E8752/1052/65, para. 18. Strang was actually reviving a suggestion made during an earlier visit to Alexandria.
49. Suggested Basis for a New Approach by the Conciliation Commission to the Parties on their Resumption of Work on the 18th July, 9 July 1949, PRO FO371/75350 E8393/1017/31; Morris, *Birth*, 272f. Shiffer mistakenly refers to this document, signed by Bevin on 11 July, as the "result" — rather than the starting-point — of "close, high-level

British-US consultations regarding the shape of the much hoped-for settlement." "The 1949 Israeli Offer" 14, 18.

50. FO to UKEmb Washington, 12 July 1949 (tgm.7008), PRO FO371/75350 E8393/1017/31; Acheson to USEmb UK, 13 July 1949, *FRUS 1949* VI, 1223f.; Douglas to Acheson, 15 July 1949 (tgm.2790), USNA 501.BB Pal/7-1549 (discussed in ibid., 1229 n.4); Acheson to USEmb Israel, 10 Aug. 1949 (tgm.510), USNA 501.BB Pal/8-149.
51. E.g., Millar to FO, 14 July 1949 (tgm.3572), PRO FO371/75350 E8636/1017/31; FO to UKEmb Washington, 23 July 1949 (tgm.7309), FO371/75350 E8789/1017/31; Troutbeck to FO, 16 July 1949 (tgm.346), FO371/75350 E8704/1017/31.
52. Acheson to USEmb UK, 1 Aug. 1949, *FRUS 1949* VI, 1275.
53. Douglas to Acheson, 4 Aug. 1949, *FRUS 1949* VI, 1285.
54. Acheson to USEmb UK, 7 Aug. 1949, *FRUS 1949* VI, 1289.
55. (Final?) revised text in FO to UKEmb Paris, 8 Aug. 1949 (tgm.2176), PRO FO371/75351 E9411/1017/31; reprinted in *FRUS 1949* VI, 1345f. and Ilan Pappé, *Britain and the Arab-Israeli Conflict, 1948-51,* (London: Macmillan Press/St. Antony's College, 1988), 215f. For reactions, see PRO FO371/75351, files E9908, E10201, E10056, E10699 and E10800/1017/31.
56. See, e.g., FO to Damascus, 28 July 1949 (tgm.525), PRO FO371/75350 E9048/1017/31; Burrows, brief for Bevin talks with Turkish Minister for Foreign Affairs, Paris, 1 Nov. 1949, FO371/75067 E13727/1052/65; Pappé, *Britain*, 122, 187.

Chapter 9

1. Shiloah to Sharett, 31 July 1949, *ID4*, 268 [D164]; cf. *ID4*, 269f., 295f., 298f., 338 n.6, 393.
2. E.g., *FRUS 1949* VI, 1291 n.2, 1297f., 1321; *ID4*, 368f., 393; Morris, *Birth*, 283.
3. Acheson to USLeg Syria, 22 July 1949, *FRUS 1949* VI, 1245f.; Hare remarks, reported in *ID4*, 274; Rabinovich, *Road Not Taken*, 80. Cf. ibid., ch.3; Shlaim, "Husni Za'im;" Pappé, *Making*, 226-28.
4. See, e.g., Sharett to Shiloah and Sasson, 7 Aug. 1949, *ID4*, 299 [D187]. Cf. ibid., 300f., 338f., 390f.; Ben-Gurion, *Yoman ha-Milhama*, 993f. (9, 26 July 1949).
5. Gabbay, *Political Study*, 247-55.
6. Rockwell to Acheson, 20 July 1949, *FRUS 1949* VI, 1238f.
7. See, e.g., meeting between Syrian and Lebanese Prime Ministers (5 Aug.), reported in Sasson to Sharett, 14 Aug. 1949, *ID4*, 333 [D208]. Cf.

Shiloah to Sharett, 15 Aug. 1949, *ID4*, 345f. [D214]; Shiloah to Eban, 1 Nov. 1949, *ID4*, 589 [D379].

8. Mulqi remarks, quoted in Kirkbride to FO, 15 Aug. 1949 (monthly report for July), PRO FO371/75273 E10169/1013/80; Sasson to Sharett, 29 Aug. 1949, *ID4*, 403 [D250]; Shlaim, *Collusion*, 481f., 487f.
9. Views of Hawwari, reported in Sasson to Sharett, 11 Aug. 1949, *ID4*, 314 [D199]; Shlaim, *Collusion*, 503f.
10. See, e.g., views of Fa'iz al-Khuri at a meeting with SD officials, 15 Aug. 1949, *FRUS 1949* VI, 1310f.; views of new Syrian foreign minister, reported in Harrison to Acheson, 19 Aug. 1949 (tgm.491), USNA 501.BB Pal/8-1949.
11. Shiloah to Sharett, 11 Aug. 1949, discussed in *ID4*, 314 n.4.
12. Ben-Gurion diary, BGA, 18 July 1949; Segev, *1949*, 40; Shlaim, *Collusion*, 465, 511.
13. Ben-Gurion, *Yoman ha-Milhama*, 993 (14 July 1949); also Sasson's view, loc.cit. (9 July). This entry has been much quoted: Segev, *1949*, 34; Shlaim, "Husni Za'im," 77; Morris, *Birth*, 282; Pappé, *Making*, 240; Rabinovich, *Road Not Taken*, 56.
14. Sharett speech to Mapai secretariat, 28 July 1949, quoted in Segev, *1949*, 40. Cf. Rabinovich, *Road Not Taken*, 57, where Sharett's position is shown to be more ambiguous; Pappé, *Making*, 232f., 234.
15. On US pressure at this time, see, e.g., Gazit, "Ben-Gurion's 1949 Proposal," 229, 238. Shiloah, who had been in Washington in late June, reported on Truman's newfound sympathy for the suffering of the Palestinian refugees. See: Ben-Gurion Diary, 30 June 1949, BGA; Segev, *1949*, 35.
16. Porter to Acheson, 28 July 1949, *FRUS 1949* VI, 1266; Shiloah to Sharett, 29 July 1949, *ID4*, 264f. [D162]; Pappé, *Making*, 228.
17. Shiloah to Azcárate, 29 July 1949, reported in Porter to Acheson, 30 July 1949, *FRUS 1949* VI, 1271. Cf. Shiloah to Sharett, 29 July 1949, *ID4*, 265 [D162]; UN Conciliation Commission for Palestine, *Fourth Progress Report* ... Covering the Period from 9 June to 15 September 1949 (UN Doc.A/992), para. 7.
18. Porter to Acheson, 30 July 1949, *FRUS 1949* VI, 1272; same to same, 2 Aug. 1949, ibid., 1276; *Falastin*, 7 Aug. 1949, p.1; PCC, *Fourth Progress Rpt.*, para.8.
19. Reports of the meeting in: Shiloah to Sharett, 3 Aug. 1949, *ID4*, 279f. [D174]; Porter to Acheson, 3 Aug. 1949, *FRUS 1949* VI, 1281f.; PCC, *Fourth Progress Rpt.*, para.9; Morris, *Birth*, 283. For another account of Israel's various proposals submitted after the recess, see Gabbay, *Political Study*, 255f.

20. For a detailed study of the tactical motives behind Israel's offer, see Shiffer, "The 1949 Israeli Offer." Cf. *ID4*, 207-60 *passim*; Gazit, "Ben-Gurion's 1949 Proposal," 238f.; Morris, *Birth*, 265f., 277-80; Pappé, *Making*, 230f.
21. See, e.g., Elath to Sharett, two telegrams dated 28 July 1949, *ID4*, 261-63 [D159, D160]; same to Eytan, 3 Aug. 1949, *ID4*, 283-85 [D177]; Sharett to Eliash, 3 Aug. 1949, *ID4*, 282 [D176].
22. Burdett to Acheson, 2 Aug. 1949, *FRUS 1949* VI, 1276f.; Morris, *Birth*, 283.
23. Acheson to USDel Lausanne, 11 Aug. 1949, *FRUS 1949* VI, 1297.
24. E.g., *ID4*, 262, 289, 308-10, 321, 334; *FRUS 1949* VI, 1261-64, 1297; UKEmb Washington to USSD, 1 Sept. 1949, *FRUS 1949* VI, 1344; Gabbay, *Political Study*, 257; Forsythe, *Peacemaking*, 56f.; Morris, *Birth*, 283.
25. Sharett to Shiloah, 10 Aug. 1949, *ID4*, 313 [D198]; Morris, *Birth*, 283.
26. Sharett, at an IMFA consultation on 31 Jan. 1950, referred to the "100,000 offer" as amounting, in reality, to 70,000. Israel State Archives, *Documents on the Foreign Policy of Israel,* Yehoshua Freundlich (ed.), vol.5 (1950), (Jerusalem: 1988), 84 [D62] (hereinafter: *ID5*).
27. Morris, *Birth*, 280-83; Sharett to Eliash, 3 Aug. 1949, *ID4*, 282 [D176]; Sharett to Shiloah and Sasson, 7 Aug. 1949, *ID4*, 298f. [D187]; Ford (Tel Aviv) to Acheson, 9 Aug. 1949, *FRUS 1949* VI, 1292; Burdett (Jerusalem) to Acheson, 16 Aug. 1949, ibid., 1319f.; Ford to Acheson, 19 Aug. 1949 (tgm.640), USNA 501.BB Pal/8-1949; Gabbay, *Political Study*, 256; Shlaim, *Collusion*, 473; Pappé, *Making*, 215.
28. Porter to Acheson, 5 Aug. 1949, *FRUS 1949* VI, 1287f.; Shiloah to Sharett, 5 Aug. 1949, *ID4*, 289 [D180]; PCC, *Fourth Progress Rpt.*, para.10; Azcárate, *Mission*, 151f.; Morris, *Birth*, 283; Shlaim, *Collusion*, 473.
29. Report of PCC private meeting with Arab delegates, 15[?] Aug., in Rockwell to Acheson, 16 Aug. 1949, *FRUS 1949* VI, 1319; same to same, 16 Aug. 1949 (tgm.PALUN280), USNA 501.BB Pal/8-1649; PCC, *Fourth Progress Rpt.*, para. 10.; Gabbay, *Political Study*, 257; Forsythe, *Peacemaking*, 57f.
30. Rockwell to Acheson, 10 Sept. 1949, *FRUS 1949* VI, 1375; ibid., 1110, 1237, 1311-13, 1328-32; *ID4*, 392, 396; McGhee, *Envoy*, 37; Shlaim, *Collusion*, 472; Pappé, *Making*, 221.
31. Yaacov Bar-Siman-Tov, "The Limits of Economic Sanctions: The American-Israeli Case of 1953," *Jnl. of Contemporary History* 23 (1988), 425-43.

32. See, e.g., Gazit, "Ben-Gurion's 1949 Proposal," 242.
33. Sharett to Elath, 25 Aug. 1949, *ID4*, 395 [D242].
34. Elath to Sharett, 25 Aug. 1949, *ID4*, 397 [D244]; Hare, memorandum of conversation (Elath, McGhee, McDonald), 25 Aug. 1949, *FRUS 1949* VI, 1328-31.
35. Darwaza, *al-Qadiyya*, 257. Cf. *FRUS 1949* VI, 1375, 1388; *ID4*, 400, 465-68.

Chapter 10

1. See, e.g., *ID4*, 255f., 258, 269f., 398f.; *FRUS 1949* VI, 1264f.; Azcárate, *Mission*, 152.
2. *FRUS 1949* VI, 1298; *ID4*, 335; Azcárate, *Mission*, 152f.; Forsythe, *Peacemaking*, 58f. Abd al-Shafi Labbaneh, a member of the Egyptian delegation, was named as the Arab member of the committee. For a discussion of the secondary questions discussed at Lausanne, see Gabbay, *Political Study*, 261f.
3. Porter to Acheson, 26 July 1949, *FRUS 1949* VI, 1254f.
4. Acheson to USDel Lausanne, 28 July 1949, *FRUS 1949* VI, 1267.
5. Porter to Acheson, two telegrams dated 5 Aug. 1949, *FRUS 1949* VI, 1286-89; Rockwell to Acheson, 11 Aug. 1949, ibid., 1299f. Pappé (*Making*, 228f.) suggests that the French and Turkish proposals were actually submitted to (and rejected by) the Arab and Israeli delegations, but this researcher has seen no evidence to support this.
6. Acheson to USDel Lausanne, two telegrams dated 11 Aug. 1949, *FRUS 1949* VI, 1297f. and 1301f.
7. Darwaza, *al-Qadiyya*, 257f.
8. Shiloah to Sharett, 9 Aug. 1949, *ID4*, 303 [D191]; ibid., 303 n.1, 314 n.3, 315, 334, 336; Forsythe, *Peacemaking*, 55f. Israelis learned of some of the internal PCC discussions from the French representative, Claude de Boisanger.
9. E.g., Acheson to USDel Lausanne, 28 July 1949, *FRUS 1949* VI, 1267; Porter to Acheson, 29 July 1949 (tgm.PALUN255), USNA 501.BB Pal/7-2949 (discussed in ibid., 1273 n.1); Rockwell to Acheson, 11 Aug. 1949, ibid., 1299.
10. Shuqayri, *Arba'un Aman*, 309.
11. Shuqayri, *Arba'un Aman*, 314; de Boisanger's report of talks with Arab delegates, in Sasson to Sharett, 26 July 1949, *ID4*, 248 [D148]; Rockwell to Acheson, 11 Aug. 1949, *FRUS 1949* VI, 1299; Shlaim, *Collusion*, 482 (citing Fawzi al-Mulqi).

12. Porter to Acheson, 29 July 1949 (tgm.PALUN255), USNA 501.BB Pal/7-2949; Shiloah to Sharett, 29 July 1949, *ID4*, 264 [D162].
13. Eban to Shiloah, 5 Aug. 1949, *ID4*, 292 [D182]; Eban to Cordier, 11 Aug. 1949, *ID4*, 322f. [D203].
14. Eban to Eytan, 8 June 1949, *ID4*, 101 [D63]; Pappé, *Making*, 225.
15. Eytan to Shiloah, 9 Aug. 1949, *ID4*, 308 [D193].
16. See, e.g., *ID4*, 315, 345f., 426, 441, 445.
17. Sasson to Sharett, 30 Sept. 1949, *ID4*, 518 [D316].
18. See, e.g., *ID4*, 202, 218, 248.
19. Eban to Shiloah, 28 July 1949, *ID4*, 260 [D158].
20. McDonald to Acheson, 26 July 1949 (tgm.566), USNA 501.BB Pal/7-2649; cf. *FRUS 1949* VI, 1245 n.2.
21. Rockwell to Acheson, 11 Aug. 1949, *FRUS 1949* VI, 1299; *ID4*, 430, 441.
22. Quoted in NSC paper NSC 47/2, 17 Oct. 1949, *FRUS 1949* VI, 1438.
23. Elath to Clifford, 15 Aug. 1949, *ID4*, 352-57 [D217]; Burdett to Acheson, 16 Aug. 1949, *FRUS 1949* VI, 1320f.
24. See, e.g., de Boisanger-Sasson conversation, reported in Sasson to Sharett, 20 Aug. 1949, *ID4*, 376 [D230]. For an Israeli analysis of Arab motives in favor of continuing the talks, see same to same, 26 Aug. 1949, *ID4*, 399 [D246].
25. McGhee, memorandum of conversation with Charles Malik, 8 July 1949, *FRUS 1949* VI, 1212. See also Barazi-Keeley talks, reported in Keeley to Acheson, 18 July 1949, *FRUS 1949* VI, 1234, and same to same, 25 July 1949 (tgm.408), USNA 501.MA Pal/7-2549.
26. See, e.g., talk with Iraqi minister to Egypt, reported in BMEO Cairo to FO, 10 March 1949 (tgm.27 Saving), PRO FO371/75332 E3335/1015/31; Khashaba views, reported in Campbell to Bevin, 12 March 1949 (desp.152 — 1/104/49G), FO371/75332 E3476/1015/31.
27. Tomkins (Strasbourg) to Burrows, 13 Aug. 1949 (tgm.23) PRO FO371/75351 E9908/1017/31. Cf. Shuqayri, *Arba'un Aman*, 314.
28. Cordier report of conversation with Fawzi (16 Aug.), in Eban to Shiloah, 18 Aug. 1949, *ID4*, 367 [D223]. Cf. Lie-Fawzi talks, reported in Rafael to Sharett, 19 Aug. 1949, *ID4*, 374 [D228]; Patterson to Acheson, 24 Aug. 1949 (Airg.A-896), USNA 501.BB Pal/8-2449.
29. Sasson and Shiloah to Sharett, 21 Aug. 1949, *ID4*, 381 [D232]; Sasson to Sharett, 29 Aug. 1949, *ID4*, 403 [D250]; Rabinovich, *Road Not Taken*, 182f.
30. Eban to Cordier, 11 Aug. 1949, *ID4*, 323-26 [D203]. Unless otherwise noted, quotations in this and the following paragraph are taken from this letter.

31. Text of Bunche report to UNSC, 4 Aug. 1949, in Medzini, *Israel's Foreign Relations*, 207f. Cf. *ID4*, 361f.
32. Eban to Elath, 11 Aug. 1949, *ID4*, 326f. [D204]; cf. Elath to Clifford, 15 Aug. 1949, *ID4*, 356 [D217].
33. Eban to Sharett, 17 Aug. 1949, *ID4*, 364f. [D220]; Eban to Perm. Rep. of Turkey, UN, 18 Aug. 1949, *ID4*, 371-73 [D227]. For the text of UNSC resolution 73, which found "that the Armistice Agreements constitute an important step toward the establishment of permanent peace in Palestine," see: Tomeh, *United Nations Resolutions*, 131f.; *ID4*, 361f.; *FRUS 1949* VI, 1302f.

Chapter 11

1. Memorandum encl. in Sasson to Sharett, 15 Aug. 1949, *ID4*, 340-42 [D213]. Cf. *FRUS 1949* VI, 1313f.; Gabbay, *Political Study*, 258f.; Hawwari, *Sirr al-Nakba*, 364f.; Forsythe, *Peacemaking*, 59f.; Pappé, *Making*, 234f.
2. Rockwell to Acheson, 15 Aug. 1949, discussed in *FRUS 1949* VI, 1314 n.1.
3. McGhee memorandum (to Acheson), Palestine Conciliation Commission, 16 Aug. 1949, *FRUS 1949* VI, 1315f.; Acheson to Certain Diplomatic and Consular Offices, 16 Aug. 1949, ibid., 1317f. On the establishment and work of the ESM, see: Gabbay, *Political Study*, 263-65; Azcárate, *Mission*, 154-56, 192-96, 199-201; Forsythe, *Peacemaking*, 61f., 68f.; Khouri, "United Nations Peace Efforts," 38-41; Touval, *Peace Brokers*, 84; Morris, *Birth*, 283-85; Ilan Pappé, "Britain and the Palestinian Refugees, 1948-50," *Middle East Focus* 9:2 (Fall 1986), 20-25; Pappé, *Making*, 229, 235-37.
4. Report of Porter's Paris meeting of 22 Aug., *FRUS 1949* VI, 1316 n.4; ibid., 1377.
5. Feinberg, report (18 Aug.) of meeting with Porter, 16 Aug. 1949, *ID4*, 226 [D226]. On Porter's emphasis on the economic aspect, see also Gabbay, *Political Study*, 258 (esp. n.138), 262f.
6. Shiloah to Sharett, 15 Aug. 1949, *ID4*, 346f. [D214].
7. Tenney to Acheson, 20 Aug. 1949 (tgm.432), USNA 501.BB Pal/8-2049; same to same, 31 Aug. 1949 (tgm.450), USNA 501.BB Pal/8-3149. Cf. Patterson to Acheson, 24 Aug. 1949 (Airg.A-896), USNA 501.BB Pal/8-2449; *FRUS 1949* VI, 1359 n.1.
8. Burdett to Acheson, 22 Aug. 1949 (tgm.526), USNA 501.BB Pal/8-2249; cf. *FRUS 1949* VI, 1326.
9. Which was — Beith added — "exactly what [the] Israelis desire[d]."

Douglas-Beith talk, reported in Douglas to Acheson, 23 Aug. 1949 (tgm.3351), USNA 501.BB Pal/8-2349; cf. *FRUS 1949* VI, 1326f.
10. *FRUS 1949* VI, 1327, 1346-48.
11. Sasson to Sharett, 26 Aug. 1949, *ID4*, 397f. [D245]. Cf. same to same, 30 Aug. 1949, *ID4*, 406 [D252], which gives 29 Aug. as the date at which this decision was made.
12. E.g., de Boisanger-Sasson conversation, reported in Sasson to Sharett, 20 Aug. 1949, *ID4*, 376f. [D230]; same to same, 26 Aug. 1949, *ID4*, 398 [D245].
13. Israeli memorandum of 23 Aug., referred to in Ford to Acheson, 29 Aug. 1949, *FRUS 1949* VI, 1335. On improved US-Israel relations at this time, see *ID4*, 393, 397.
14. Memorandum AR/17, 29 Aug. 1949, summary in *FRUS 1949* VI, 1337f.; Hawwari, *Sirr al-Nakba*, 365f.; Gabbay, *Political Study*, 266; Forsythe, *Peacemaking*, 60.
15. Hawwari, *Sirr al-Nakba*, 367-70; Sasson to Sharett, 29 Aug. 1949, *ID4*, 404 [D250]; Shlaim, *Collusion*, 505.
16. Shiloah to de Boisanger, 31 Aug. 1949 (UN Doc. IS/36), *ID4*, 417-20 [D255], summary in *FRUS 1949* VI, 1349f. Cf. Forsythe, *Peacemaking*, 60; Gabbay, *Political Study*, 259f.
17. Rockwell to Acheson, 2 Sept. 1949, *FRUS 1949* VI, 1354f.
18. de Boisanger to Head of IsrDel, 5 Sept. 1949, *ID4*, 432-35 [D265]; Sasson-Rockwell talk, reported in Sasson to Sharett, 5 Sept. 1949, *ID4*, 430f. [D262]; *FRUS 1949* VI, 1361f.; Pappé, *Making*, 237f.
19. Rockwell to Acheson, 6 Sept. 1949 (tgm.PALUN305), USNA 501.BB Pal/9-649 (cf. *FRUS 1949* VI, 1362 n.1); same to same, 5 Sept. 1949, *FRUS 1949* VI, 1362; Sasson-Rockwell talk, reported in Sasson to Sharett, 6 Sept. 1949, *ID4*, 436f. [D267].
20. Rockwell to Acheson, 2 Sept. 1949, *FRUS 1949* VI, 1354f.
21. Acheson to USDel Lausanne, 8 Sept. 1949, *FRUS 1949* VI, 1369.
22. Sasson talks with Azcárate, Rockwell, de Boisanger and Mustafa (4-8 Sept.), reported in *ID4*, 426, 430f., 440-42, 446; Pappé, *Making*, 238.
23. PCC Note to IsrDel, 12 Sept. 1949, *ID4*, 455-58 [D281]. Cf. Rockwell summary of notes and meeting with delegations, 14 Sept. 1949, *FRUS 1949* VI, 1387f.; Gabbay, *Political Study*, 260.
24. Acheson to USEmb Paris and Ankara, 17 Sept. 1949, *FRUS 1949* VI, 1392.
25. Pappé, *Making*, 237.
26. PCC, *Fourth Progress Rpt.*, quoted in *FRUS 1949* VI, 1388.
27. Sharett to Eban, 26 Sept. 1949, *ID4*, 495f. [D306]; Sasson to Sharett, 28

Sept. 1949, *ID4*, 502f. [D310]; same to same, 30 Sept. 1949, *ID4*, 517-20 [D316]; Shlaim, *Collusion*, 511; Pappé, *Making*, 238.

Chapter 12

1. Acheson to certain diplomatic and consular offices, 14 Oct. 1949, *FRUS 1949* VI, 1428-30.
2. Austin to Acheson, 19 Oct. 1949, *FRUS 1949* VI, 1447f.; Webb to Truman, 26 Oct. 1949, ibid., 1455.
3. The Jerusalem subcommittee of the PCC had proposed, on 1 Sept., a draft Statute for Jerusalem, and the Israelis had begun transferring government ministries there. There was also, at this time, an increase in direct Israel-Jordan contacts in an attempt to coordinate their respective positions against the internationalization of the city. See, e.g.: *FRUS 1949* VI, 1356f., 1366f., 1396f., 1419f., 1440f.; 1445f., 1524f., 1528-38 *passim*; *ID4*, 553-56, 635f., 727; McDonald, *My Mission*, ch.xviii; Azcárate, *Mission*, 156f.; Forsythe, *Peacemaking*, 65-67; Shlaim, *Collusion*, ch.17.
4. Mulqi quoted in PCC memorandum (AR/56) to Arab delegations, Paris, 4 Oct. 1951, copy in PRO FO371/91366 EE1071/46. Cf. PCC, *Eighth Progress Report* ... Covering the Period from 11 December 1949 to 23 October 1950 (UN Doc.A/1367/Rev.1) 5 GAOR Suppl. No.18, 1-21, 30-31 (2 Sept. and 23 Oct. 1950), para. 22 (cited hereinafter as PCC, *Eighth Progress Rpt.*); *ID4*, 631.
5. Report of meeting in Austin to Acheson, 24 Oct. 1949, *FRUS 1949* VI, 1450f. For another view of the Arab states' mood and attitude to the PCC at this time, see Shuqayri, *Arba'un Aman*, 314f.
6. Eban to Sharett, 21 Oct. 1949, *ID4*, 568 [D362]. Cf. Forsythe, *Peacemaking*, 63f.
7. Eban to Yalçin, 27 Oct. 1949, *ID4*, 578-82 [D372]. Quotations in this and the following paragraphs are from this letter. A summary of Eban's letter is given in PCC, *Eighth Progress Rpt.*, para. 23. See also Israel government memorandum to PCC, 31 March 1950, *ID5*, 228 [D164].
8. Yalçin to Eban, 15 Nov. 1949, *ID4*, 630 [D414]; PCC, *Eighth Progress Rpt.*, paras. 13-14. For his part, however, PCC secretary (Azcárate, *Mission*, 150f.) tended to share the more restrictive and procedural Israeli interpretation.
9. See, e.g., Sasson to Sherine, 8 Nov. 1949, transl. in PRO FO371/75345 E14875/1016/31G; Rabinovich, *Road Not Taken*, 115.
10. Meeting between PCC members and staff at the USSD, 3 Nov. 1949, *FRUS 1949* VI, 1466. Cf. *ID4*, 602, 616. For the PCC's lengthy reply, see Yalçin to Eban, 15 Nov. 1949 (Doc.IS/42), *ID4*, 627-32 [D414].

11. Elath to Sharett, 9 Nov. 1949, *ID4*, 616 [D404].
12. The Iraqis cited Ambassador Jessup's remarks at the 3rd UNGA in Paris, President Truman's letter to King Abdallah of 28 March 1949, and various remarks by Mark Ethridge and Raymond Hare to the Arab delegations at Lausanne.
13. Iraq MFA to USEmb Baghdad, *aide-mémoire* (1450/696/13), 8 Nov. 1949, copy in PRO FO371/75355 E14455/1017/31; cf. *FRUS 1949* VI, 1488 n.2.
14. Memorandum of conversation between Webb, McGhee, Stabler and diplomatic representatives of Egypt, Saudi Arabia, Jordan, Lebanon, Syria, Iraq and Yemen, 14 Nov. 1949, *FRUS 1949* VI, 1486-88; memorandum submitted by Arab representatives to Acheson, 14 Nov. 1949, ibid., 1488-90.
15. Elath to Sharett, 14 Nov. 1949, *ID4*, 624 [D411]; James Reston, "Arabs Ask US Aid in Palestine Issue," The *New York Times*, 15 Nov. 1949, pp. 1,8.
16. *FRUS 1949* VI, 1487.
17. For proposals to abolish or replace the PCC at this time, see, e.g.: Forsythe, *Peacemaking*, 65, 69; Azcárate, *Mission*, 157f.
18. Statement by the United States and the United Kingdom Groups: Discussion on a Palestine Settlement, 14 Nov. 1949, *FRUS 1949* VI, 65. Cf. McGhee, *Envoy*, 53-59.

Chapter 13

1. Shwadran, "Palestine Conciliation Commission," 275, 285; Shlaim, *Collusion*, 461f.
2. McDonald to Acheson, 20 June 1950, United States, Department of State, *Foreign Relations of the United States: 1950*, vol. V, (Washington 1978), (hereinafter: *FRUS 1950* V), 935f.
3. Khouri, "United Nations Peace Efforts," 27 (cf. ibid., 89); Touval, *Peace Brokers*, 76f.; Forsythe, *Peacemaking*, 35.
4. Touval, *Peace Brokers*, ch.4.
5. Morris, *Birth*, 285. Cf. Shlaim, *Collusion*, 465.
6. Gershon Avner, interview in Shlaim, *Collusion*, 463f.
7. Touval, *Peace Brokers*, 91, 104.
8. PCC, Supplementary report to *Eighth Progress Rpt.*, 23 Oct. 1950, para. 3, reproduced in Moore, *The Arab-Israeli Conflict*, III: 539.
9. Eban to Sharett, 26 June 1950, *ID5*, 406 [D291].
10. Hawwari, *Sirr al-Nakba*, 361f.
11. Sasson to Divon, 16 June 1949, *ID4*, 135-37 [D81]; Shlaim, *Collusion*,

473-76; Morris, *Birth*, 276f.; Pappé, *Making*, 240f. For other internal critiques of Israel's improvisation and lack of a clear policy, see, e.g.: Eytan to Sharett, 3 May 1949, *ID4*, 11 [D4]; Rafael to Eban, 8 July 1949, *ID4*, 213-15 [D130]; Shlaim, *Collusion*, 493, 502f.

12. Shlaim, *Collusion*, 511f., citing Avraham Sela, *Mi-Maga'im le-Masa u-Matan: Yihasei ha-Sokhnut ha-Yehudit u-Medinat Yisrael 'im ha-Melekh Abdallah, 1946-1950* (From Contacts to Negotiations: Relations Between the Jewish Agency and the State of Israel with King Abdallah), Tel Aviv: Shiloah Institute of Tel Aviv University, 1985; Rabinovich, *Road Not Taken*, 58.
13. Pappé, *Making*, 225.
14. Pappé, *Making*, 210.
15. Gabbay, *Political Study*, 273. Cf. Shlaim, *Collusion*, 466.
16. Eytan to Eban, 13 June 1949, *ID4*, 128f. [D75].
17. Cf. Shlaim, *Collusion*, 488.
18. Cf. Touval, *Peace Brokers*, 86-89; Khouri, "United Nations Peace Efforts," 32.
19. Shlaim, *Collusion*, 461f.
20. Ben-Gurion Diary, 18 July 1949, BGA; Shlaim, *Collusion*, 511.
21. Shuqayri, *Arba'un Aman*, 308.
22. Shlaim, *Collusion*, 462. Cf. Gazit, "Mediation and Mediators," 87f.; *ID4*, 441, 445, 616-18.
23. Cf. Touval, *Peace Brokers*, 89, where the disagreement between the US and France regarding Jerusalem is also mentioned.
24. Shiloah to Sharett, 15 Aug. 1949, *ID4*, 345 [D214]; Eytan to Sharett, 3 May 1949, *ID4*, 13 [D4]. Cf. Barco to Acheson, 22 June 1950, *FRUS 1950* V, 938f.; Azcárate, *Mission*, 166.
25. Touval, *Peace Brokers*, 95, 104. Cf. Rabinovich, *Road Not Taken*, 55.
26. Franks (Washington) to FO, 30 Aug. 1950 (tgm.556 Saving), PRO FO371/82196 EE10110/47.
27. Gazit, "Mediation and Mediators," 86. Cf. Azcárate, *Mission*, 134, 145f., 164.
28. Shwadran, "Palestine Conciliation Commission," 281.
29. Gazit, "Mediation and Mediators," 87.
30. *FRUS 1949* VI, 1429.
31. Azcárate, *Mission*, 134-80 *passim*; McDonald to Acheson, 20 June 1950, *FRUS 1950* V, 935f.; McDonald, *My Mission*, 176f. Cf. Touval, *Peace Brokers*, 89f.; Shlaim, *Collusion*, 462; Khouri, "United Nations Peace Efforts," 32f.
32. Shuqayri, *Arba'un Aman*, 310, 314; Hawwari, *Sirr al-Nakba*, 361.

33. Eban to Sharett, 27 April 1949, *ID2*, 594 [D511].
34. Eban to Elath, 11 Aug. 1949, *ID4*, 327 [D204]; Najar to Eytan, 14 Aug. 1949, *ID4*, 338 [D212]; Azcárate, *Mission*, 137, 154; Khouri, "United Nations Peace Efforts," 33.
35. See Fischer to Avner, 21 Dec. 1949, *ID4*, 754f. [D513].
36. Shuqayri, *Arba'un Aman*, 310; talk with Ethridge (1 April), reported in Houstoun Boswall (Beirut) to FO, 2 April 1949 (tgm.196), PRO FO371/75340 E4318/1016/31G.
37. Talk with Yalçin (31 March), reported in Houstoun Boswall (Beirut) to FO, 1 April 1949 (tgm.193), PRO FO371/75349 E4281/1017/31.
38. Hawwari, *Sirr al-Nakba*, 361.
39. Touval, *Peace Brokers*, 92f.
40. Halderman, memorandum of conversation (Riley, Hare, Berry, Wilkins, Rockwell), 11 July 1950, *FRUS 1950* V, 949; Kirkbride to FO, 31 Aug. 1950 (tgm.300), PRO FO371/82196 EE10110/46.
41. Bunche-Riley-Cordier-Jebb meeting, 1 Aug., reported in Jebb (UN, New York) to Bevin, 3 Aug. 1950 (desp.30, 52/12/50P), PRO FO371/82196 EE10110/38.
42. Gazit, "Mediation and Mediators," 86.
43. Shlaim, *Collusion*, 462-65; Forsythe, *Peacemaking*, 71. Cf. ibid., 42f.; Touval, *Peace Brokers*, 93f.
44. Nadav Safran, quoted in Touval, *Peace Brokers*, 79. Cf. Gazit, "Mediation and Mediators," 86f.
45. See, e.g., Eytan, *The First Ten Years*, 31, 51-53; Gazit, "Mediation and Mediators," 86f.; Touval, *Peace Brokers*, 79.
46. Azcárate, *Mission*, 148f.; Gershon Avner interview, quoted in Shlaim, *Collusion*, 463f.
47. PCC, *Eighth Progress Rpt.*, paras. 6, 7, 11.
48. Azcárate, *Mission*, 149. At the State Department, Raymond Hare took a similar line against such criticisms of the PCC. See Halderman, memorandum of conversation (Riley, Hare, Berry, Wilkins, Rockwell), 11 July 1950, *FRUS 1950* V, 949.
49. Touval, *Peace Brokers*, 94.
50. See, e.g., Azcárate, *Mission*, 149.
51. Gazit, "Mediation and Mediators," 87.
52. Azcárate, *Mission*, 136-38.
53. Forsythe, *Peacemaking*, 65.
54. Barry Rubin, *Secrets of State: The State Department and the Struggle Over US Foreign Policy*, (Oxford/New York: Oxford University Press, 1985), vii.

55. *FRUS 1949* VI, 174; McDonald, *My Mission*, 200.
56. Acheson to Egyptian Ambassador (*et al.*), 13 Dec. 1949, *FRUS 1949* VI, 1535f.
57. Recapitulation of Conclusions for Confidential Guidance of Chiefs of Mission in Oral Presentation to Governments, *FRUS 1949* VI, 177; Comay report of talks with McDonald, in Comay to Elath, 5 Dec. 1949, *ID4*, 684 [D460]; McDonald, *My Mission*, 202.
58. Azcárate, *Mission*, 137f. Cf. ibid., 146, 164, 166; Khouri, "United Nations Peace Efforts," 33f.; Forsythe, *Peacemaking*, 36, 52.
59. Touval, *Peace Brokers*, 94f., 104.
60. Touval, *Peace Brokers*, 97-100, 102f.
61. Pappé, *Making*, 225.
62. Touval, *Peace Brokers*, 83, 98f.; Morris, *Birth*, 279, 281.
63. Rabinovich, *Road Not Taken*, 57.
64. This view was shared by Israeli officials at the time. See, e.g., Lourie-Ross meeting, 19 July 1950, *ID5*, 438 [D319].
65. Touval, *Peace Brokers*, 79f.
66. NSC 47/2, 17 Oct. 1949, *FRUS 1949* VI, 1438.
67. Morris, *Birth*, 259f., 277f.
68. Forsythe, *Peacemaking*, 53. Cf. McDonald, *My Mission*, 182-84.
69. Forsythe, *Peacemaking*, 70.
70. Shiffer, "The 1949 Israeli Offer," 18. See also: Sharett remarks, IMFA consultation, 31 Jan. 1950, *ID5*, 84 [D62]; Shlaim, *Collusion*, 473f.; Morris, *Birth*, 282; Rabinovich, *Road Not Taken*, 57.
71. Morris, *Birth*, 285.
72. Morris, *Birth*, 285.
73. Khouri, "United Nations Peace Efforts," 36.
74. Rabinovich, *Road Not Taken*, 26. Cf. Touval, *Peace Brokers*, 94.
75. Touval, *Peace Brokers*, 100f.
76. See, e.g., Sasson to Sharett, 3 and 4 July 1949, *ID4*, 203 [D120, D121]. Cf. Rabinovich, *Road Not Taken*, 63.
77. Touval, *Peace Brokers*, 104f.
78. Touval, *Peace Brokers*, 101 (emphasis added).
79. Statement by the United States and the United Kingdom Groups: Discussion on a Palestine Settlement, 14 Nov. 1949, *FRUS 1949* VI, 64. Cf. McGhee, *Envoy*, 53-59; Acheson to Certain Diplomatic and Consular Offices, 14 Oct. 1949, *FRUS 1949* VI, 1429.

SOURCES AND BIBLIOGRAPHY

Primary Sources

Selected American and Israeli documents on the Lausanne conference and the work of the PCC have become available in recent years thanks to two excellent official publications: the *Foreign Relations of the United States* [FRUS] series, and its Israeli counterpart, *Documents on the Foreign Policy of Israel* [Israel Documents, *ID*]. The three principal volumes of primary sources used for this study are:

FRUS 1949 VI - United States, Department of State, *Foreign Relations of the United States: Diplomatic Papers: 1949*, vol. VI, (Washington: 1977), 594-1490.

ID2 - *Documents on the Foreign Policy of Israel* vol. 2 (October 1948-April 1949), ed. Yehoshua Freundlich, (Jerusalem: 1984), 408-616.

ID4 - *Documents on the Foreign Policy of Israel* vol. 4 (May-December 1949), ed. Yemima Rosenthal, (Jerusalem: 1986), 3-582.

Another major primary source for this study is the declassified documents available at the following archives:

BGA - Ben-Gurion Archives, Sde Boqer
CZA - Central Zionist Archives, Jerusalem
ISA - Israel State Archives, Jerusalem
PRO - Public Record Office, Kew, London
UNA - United Nations Archives, New York
USNA - United States National Archives, Washington DC
WNRC - Washington National Records Center, Suitland MD

Other published primary sources are as follows:

FRUS 1950 V - United States, Department of State, *Foreign Relations of the United States: 1950*, vol.V, Washington 1978.

ID3 - Israel State Archives, *Documents on the Foreign Policy of Israel* vol. 3 (Armistice Negotiations with the Arab States: December 1948-July 1949), ed. Yemima Rosenthal, Jerusalem: 1983.

ID5 - Israel State Archives, *Documents on the Foreign Policy of Israel* vol.5 (1950) ed. Yehoshua Freundlich, Jerusalem: 1988.

The Arab-Israeli Conflict, vol. III: Documents, ed. John Norton Moore, Princeton: Princeton University Press, 1974.

The Arab States and the Arab League: A Documentary Record, vol.II International Affairs, ed. Muhammad Khalil, Beirut: Khayats, 1962.

Ben-Gurion, David, *Yoman ha-Milhama: Milhemet ha-Atzmaut* (War Diary: The War of Independence, 1947-1949), ed. Gershon Rivlin and Elhanan Orren, 3 vols., Tel Aviv: Ministry of Defense Publishing, 1982.

Israel Office of Information, *Israel's Struggle for Peace*, New York: 1960.

Israel's Foreign Relations: Selected Documents 1947-1974, ed. Meron Medzini, Jerusalem: Ministry of Foreign Affairs, 1976.

Sharett, Moshe, *Be-Shaar ha-Umot, 1946-1949* (At the Gate of the Nations), Tel Aviv: Am Oved, 1958.

United Nations Conciliation Commission for Palestine, *Third Progress Report...* Covering the Period from 9 April to 8 June 1949 U.N. Doc.A/927, 21 June, 1949.

United Nations Conciliation Commission for Palestine, *Fourth Progress Report...* Covering the Period from 9 June to 15 September 1949, U.N. Doc.A/992, 22 Sept. 1949.

United Nations Conciliation Commission for Palestine, *Eighth Progress Report...* Covering the Period from 11 December 1949 to 23 October 1950,U.N. Doc.A/1367/Rev., 5 GAOR Suppl. No. 18, 1-21, 30-1, 2 Sept. and 23 Oct. 1950.

United Nations Resolutions on Palestine and the Arab-Israeli Conflict, vol.I: 1947-1974, ed. George J. Tomeh, Washington: Institute for Palestine Studies, 1975.

Memoirs

de Azcárate, Pablo, *Mission in Palestine*, 1948-1952, Washington: Middle East Institute, 1966.

Eytan, Walter, *The First Ten Years: A Diplomatic History of Israel*, New York: Simon & Schuster, 1958.

al-Hashimi, Taha, *Mudhakirat Taha al-Hashimi,* vol. II: 1942-1955 (The Memoirs of Taha al-Hashimi), ed. Khaldun Sati al-Husri, Beirut: 1978.

al-Hawwari, Muhammad Nimr, *Sirr al-Nakba* (The Secret of the Catastrophe), Nazareth: 1955.

McDonald, James G., *My Mission in Israel, 1948-1951*, New York: Simon & Schuster, 1951.

McGhee, George, *Envoy to the Middle World: Adventures in Diplomacy*, fwd. Dean Rusk, New York: Harper & Row, 1983.

al-Shuqayri, Ahmad, *Arba'un Aman fi-l-Hayat al-Arabiyya wa'l-Duliyya* (Forty Years in Arab and International Life), Beirut: 1969.

Press

al-Ahram, Cairo, Egypt
ha-Aretz, Tel Aviv, Israel
al-Difaa, Amman, Jordan
Falastin, Jerusalem, Jordan
Jerusalem Post, Jerusalem, Israel
New York Times

Secondary Sources

Books and Theses

Abd al-Hadi, Mahdi, *al-Masala al-Filastiniyya wa-Mashariy' al-Hulul as-Siyasiyya, 1924-1974* (The Palestinian Question and Plans for Political Solutions), Beirut: 1975.

Bar-Joseph, Uri, *The Best of Enemies: Israel and Transjordan in the War of 1948*, London: Frank Cass, 1987.

Darwaza, Muhammad Izzat, *al-Qadiyya al-Filastiniyya fi Mukhtalif Marahiliha* (The Palestine Cause in its Different Phases), vol. II, Beirut: 1951 (reprinted 1960).

Forsythe, David P., *United Nations Peacemaking: The Conciliation Commission for Palestine*, Baltimore/London: Johns Hopkins University Press, 1972.

Gabbay, Rony E., *A Political Study of the Arab-Jewish Conflict: The Arab Refugee Problem: A Case Study*, Genève: Librairie E. Droz (Paris: Librairie Minard), 1959.

Louis, Wm. Roger, *The British Empire in the Middle East, 1945-1951: Arab Nationalism, The United States, and Postwar Imperialism*, Oxford: Clarendon Press, 1984.

Morris, Benny, *The Birth of the Palestinian Refugee Problem, 1947-1949*, Cambridge/New York: Cambridge University Press, 1987.

Ninberg, Ruth Levy, *ha-Emda ha-Aravit Klapei Ve'idat Lausanne, 1949* (The Arab Position at the Lausanne Conference), unpublished M.A. thesis, University of Haifa, November 1987.

Pappé, Ilan, *Britain and the Arab-Israeli Conflict, 1948-51*, London: Macmillan Press/St. Antony's College, 1988.

Pappé, Ilan, *The Making of the Arab-Israeli Conflict, 1947-51*, London/New York: I.B. Tauris, 1992.

Plascov, Avi, *The Palestinian Refugees in Jordan, 1948-1957*, London: Frank Cass, 1981.

Rabinovich, Itamar, *The Road Not Taken: Early Arab-Israeli Negotiations*, New York/Oxford: Oxford University Press, 1991.

Rubin, Barry, *Secrets of State: The State Department and the Struggle Over U.S. Foreign Policy*, Oxford/New York: Oxford University Press, 1985.

Segev, Tom, *1949: The First Israelis*, New York/London: Free Press/Collier Macmillan, 1986.

Sela, Avraham, *Mi-Maga'im le-Masa u-Matan: Yihasei ha-Sokhnut ha — Yehudit u-Medinat Yisrael 'im ha-Melekh Abdallah, 1946-1950* (From Contacts to Negotiations: Relations Between the Jewish Agency and the State of Israel with King Abdallah), Tel Aviv: Shiloah Institute of Tel Aviv University, 1985.

Shlaim, Avi, *Collusion Across the Jordan: King Abdullah, the Zionist Movement, and the Partition of Palestine*, Oxford: Clarendon Press, 1988.

Stein, Kenneth W., and Samuel W. Lewis (with Sheryl J. Brown), *Making Peace among Arabs and Israelis: Lessons from Fifty Years of Negotiating Experience*, Washington: United States Institute of Peace, October 1991.

Touval, Saadia, *The Peace Brokers: Mediators in the Arab-Israeli Conflict, 1948-1979*, Princeton: Princeton University Press, 1982.

Zuaytir, Akram, *al-Qadiyya al-Filastiniyya* (The Palestine Cause), ?Cairo: 1955.

Articles and Pamphlets

Bar-Siman-Tov, Yaacov, "The Limits of Economic Sanctions: The American-Israeli Case of 1953," *Jnl. of Contemporary History* 23 (1988), 425-43.

Cohen, Raymond, and S. Cohen, *Peace Conferences: The Formal Aspects*, Leonard Davis Institute: Jerusalem Papers on Peace Problems, Jan. 1974.

Gazit, Mordechai, "Ben-Gurion's 1949 Proposal to Incorporate the Gaza Strip with Israel," *Studies in Zionism* 8:2 (1987), 223-43.

Gazit, Mordechai, "Mediation and Mediators," *Jerusalem Journal of International Relations* 5:4 (1981), 80-104.

Khouri, Fred J., "United Nations Peace Efforts," in *The Elusive Peace in the Middle East*, ed. Malcolm H. Kerr (Albany: State University of New York Press, 1975), 19-101.

Morris, Benny, "The Crystallization of Israeli Policy Against a Return of the Arab Refugees: April-December, 1948," *Studies in Zionism* 6:1 (Spring 1985), 85-118.

Oren, Michael, "The Diplomatic Struggle for the Negev, 1946-1956," *Studies in Zionism* 10:2 (Autumn 1989), 197-215.

Pappé, Ilan, "Britain and the Palestinian Refugees, 1948-50," *Middle East Focus* 9:2 (Fall 1986), 19-25, 31.

Perla, Shlomo, "Israel and the Palestine Conciliation Commission," *Middle Eastern Studies* 26:1 (Jan. 1990), 113-18.

Shiffer, Varda, "The 1949 Israeli Offer to Repatriate 100,000 Palestinian Refugees," *Middle East Focus* 9:2 (Fall 1986), 13-18.

Shlaim, Avi, "Husni Za'im and the Plan to Resettle Palestinian Refugees in Syria," *Jnl. of Palestine Studies* 15:4 (no. 60) (Summer 1986), 68-80.

Shwadran, Benjamin, "Palestine Conciliation Commission," *Middle Eastern Affairs* (Oct. 1950), 271-85.

INDEX

Abd al-Hadi, Ibrahim, 22
Abdallah, King of Jordan, 27, 39-40, 42, 64, 80, 122, 166(n12)
Abu al-Huda, Tawfiq, 21, 27
Acheson, Dean G., 22, 26, 32-34, 36-37, 46, 61, 63, 66-68, 77, 80-82, 84, 88, 93, 96-97, 109, 111, 125, 131, 135
Ammoun, Fuad, 52
Atassi, Adnan al-, 52
Avner (see: Hirsch)
Azcárate, Pablo de, 51, 121, 129, 131-132, 165(n8)
Azm, Khalid al-, 21, 29-30
Azzam, Abd al-Rahman, 83

Barazi, Muhsin, 77
Barco, James W., 55
Ben-Gurion, David, 25-26, 30, 33-34, 36-38, 44, 60, 62, 90, 124, 143(n5)
Bernadotte, Count Folke, 14-15, 99, 118
Bevin, Ernest, 67, 92
Bilby, Kenneth, 90
Boisanger, Claude de, 46, 49, 51, 63, 100, 108, 125, 127, 143(n5), 161(n8)
Bunche, Ralph J., 16, 27, 38, 51, 91, 102, 118, 124, 127, 129
Burdett, William C., 93, 106

Campbell, Sir Ronald, 22, 82
Clapp, Gordon R., 106
Comay, Michael, 35

Douglas, Lewis W., 88
Dulles, John Foster, 94

Eban, Aubrey (Abba), 36, 43, 45, 52-53, 65, 78-79, 81, 91, 99, 100, 102-103, 112-114
Elath (Epstein), Eliahu, 36, 46, 85, 95, 102
Ethridge, Mark, 13-14, 21-27, 29-30, 32, 34-37, 40, 43-48, 50, 58-59, 61-62, 64-65, 70-74, 82, 97, 104, 118, 125, 127-128, 143(n1), 166(n12)
Eytan, Walter, 33, 44-46, 51-52, 54, 56-59, 61-64, 70-73, 78-79, 84, 99, 100, 108, 121, 123, 129, 140(n1), 154(n11)

Fawzi, Mahmud, 101
Forsythe, David P., 129, 132, 134

Gabbay, Rony E., 123
Gazit, Mordechai, 129-130, 151(n9)

Hare, Raymond A., 72-73, 75, 86, 166(n12), 168(n48)
Hassuna, Abd al-Khaliq, 81
Hawwari, Muhammad Nimr al-, 41, 121-122, 128

Heyd, Uriel, 66, 78
Hirsch (Avner), Gershon, 43, 72, 77, 89, 120

Jessup, Philip C., 13, 63, 97, 99, 100, 134, 136, 166(n12)

Keeley, James, 29
Khalil, Ahmad, 42
Khashaba, Ahmad Muhammad, 65, 68, 83
Khouri, Fred J., 132-133
Kirkbride, Sir Alec S., 129

Labbaneh, Abd al-Shafi, 161(n2)
Lovett, Robert, 13-14

Malik, Charles, 101
McDonald, James G., 60, 118
McGhee, George C., 43, 45, 61, 75-76, 85, 94-95, 105, 114, 116, 137
Morris, Benny, 93, 119, 133, 135
Mulqi, Fawzi al-, 44, 52, 59, 112
Mustafa, Abd al-Munim, 52, 65, 84, 89, 112

Palmer, Ely E., 111, 117-118
Pappé, Ilan, 122-123, 148(n28), 151(n9), 161(n5)
Patterson, Jefferson, 68, 80, 82-84
Porter, Paul A., 76, 90-91, 94, 96-98, 104-105, 111, 118, 125, 127

Quwatli, Shukri al-, 29

Rabinovich, Itamar, 136
Riley, William E., 128
Rockwell, Stuart W., 89-90, 94, 104, 107-108
Rubin, Barry, 131
Rusk, Dean, 65-66, 78

Sa'id, Nuri, 28
Safran, Nadav, 11, 129, 133
Sasson, Eliahu, 27, 41, 64, 72, 79, 91, 100, 108, 121-122, 128-129
Sharett (Shertok), Moshe, 20-21, 23-24, 26-27, 29-30, 32-33, 37-38, 40, 57, 62, 71, 73, 78-79, 84, 91-93, 95, 128, 133, 159(n14)

Shertok (see: Sharett)
Shiffer, Varda, 157-158(n49)
Shihadeh, Aziz, 41
Shiloah, Reuven, 84, 89-91, 93, 98, 100, 105, 107, 159(n15)
Shlaim, Avi, 129
Shuqayri, Ahmad al-, 30, 53-54, 121, 124, 127-128
Strang, Sir William, 87

Touval, Saadia, 118, 120, 125, 128, 130, 132-133, 136-137
Truman, Harry S., 33, 35, 60, 94, 111, 134, 159(n15), 166(n12)

Vigier, Henri, 148(n2)

Webb, James E., 65, 115, 116
Wright, Michael, 87

Yalçin, Hussein, 34, 72, 112, 125, 128

Za'im, Husni, 77, 89, 90, 148(n2)

Former Publications in the Occasional Papers Series

(E) English
(H) Hebrew

83. **B. Neuberger:** Involvement, Invasion and Withdrawal: Qadhdhafi's Libya and Chad, 1969-1981, April 1982. (E)
84. **E. Kanovsky:** The Iran-Iraq War: Its Economic Implications, May 1982. (E)
85. **E. Kanovsky:** Migration from the Poor to the Rich Arab Countries, June 1984. (E)
86. **A. Oded:** Islamic Activities of the Arab Countries in Africa, June 1984. (H)
87. **I. Rabinovich:** The Politics of Fragmentation and Anticipation: Inter-Arab Relations in the Early 1980s, October 1984. (E)
88. **G. Ben-Dor:** State, Society and Military Elites in the Middle East — An Essay in Comparative Political Sociology, October 1984. (E)
89. **E. Kanovsky:** What's Behind Syria's Current Economic Problems? May 1985. (E)
90. **E. Rekhess:** The Arab Village in Israel — A Political-National Center, May 1985. (H)
91. **R. Aviran:** The Syrian-Palestinian Conflict in Lebanon: Syrian Nationalism versus Palestinian Particularism, May 1985. (H)
92. **A. Sela:** From Contacts to Negotiations: The Jewish Agency and the State of Israel's Relationship with King Abdallah, 1946-1950, January 1986. (H)
93. **A. Oded:** Egypt in Africa: Attitudes and Developments in Mubarak's Reign, March 1986. (H)
94. **E. Kanovsky:** Saudi Arabia's Dismal Economic Future: Regional and Global Implications, April 1986. (E)
95. **S. Shapira:** Imam Musa al-Sadr and the Shi'ite Movement in Lebanon, April 1986. (H)
96. **G. Feiler:** The Number of Egyptian Workers in the Arab Oil Countries, 1974-1983: A Critical Discussion, October 1986. (E)
97. **I. Gal:** The Development of the Oil Sector in Egypt: Its Standing in the Economy and Repercussions on Egyptian Policy towards Israel, October 1986. (H)
98. **J. Goldberg & J. Kostiner (eds.):** A Decade of Recession — The Middle East in the Shadow of the Oil Decline, January 1987. (H)
99. **M. Mottale:** Iran: The Political Sociology of the Islamic Revolution, February 1987. (E)

100. **J. Ginat:** Analysis of the Arab Vote in the 1984 Elections, July 1987. (E)

101. **M. Kramer:** The Moral Logic of Hizballah, August 1987. (E)

102. **E. Tauber:** The Entry of Military Officers into Arab Politics, February 1988. (H)

103. **Sh. Bar:** The Jordanian Communist Party: An Historical Analysis, November 1988. (H)

104. **W. W. Harris:** The Christian Camp on the Eve of the 1988 Lebanese Presidential Elections, November 1988. (E)

105. **G. Biger:** The Iran-Iraq Border: Anatomy of a Borderline in the Middle East, January 1989. (H)

106. **E. Kanovsky:** Jordan's Economy: From Prosperity to Crisis, May 1989. (E)

107. **S. Teveth:** The Evolution of "Transfer" in Zionist Thinking, May 1989. (E)

109. *Soviet Studies on the Middle East;* **V. A. Isayev:** Current Issues in Inter-Arab Economic Cooperation; **V. I. Nosenko:** The Transformation of the Soviet Stand on the Palestinian Problem, January 1991. (E)

110. **D. Rachovitz:** Missed Opportunity? The Industrialization of Egypt, 1882-1914, January 1991. (H)

111. **M. Klein:** The PLO and the Intifada: Between Euphoria and Despair, 1991. (H)

112. Negotiations in the Middle East: The Lessons of Fifty Years, 1993. (H)

113. **N. Caplan:** The Lausanne Conference, 1949: A Case Study in Middle East Peacemaking, 1993. (E)

114. **D. Menashri(ed.):** Islamic Fundamentalism: A Challenge to Regional Stability, 1993. (H)

For orders please write to:
The Moshe Dayan Center, Tel Aviv University
Tel Aviv 69978 ◆ Fax: 972-3-6415802.